MOVEMENT
OF PRAYER

MOVEMENT OF PRAYER

ALICIA JACKSON

Library of Congress Control Number:		2020911156
ISBN:	Hardcover	978-1-9845-8447-2
	Softcover	978-1-9845-8446-5
	eBook	978-1-9845-8445-8

Print information available on the last page.

Rev. date: 07/09/2020

To order additional copies of this book, contact:
Xlibris
1-888-795-4274
www.Xlibris.com
Orders@Xlibris.com
814826

This book is dedicated to my parents, who are no longer with us today but who planted us as seeds in the soil and prayed daily that the seeds would grow roots and take hold. So they watered the seeds daily until one day small plants began to emerge and break through the soil. My parents never stopped watering us until God called them home.

God, I thank You for my parents, on whose minds and hearts You imprinted the command to be like You, which gave us an unforgettable and unshakable foundation. They are gone but not forgotten, and words can't describe the love for them I carry inside and the memories that remain continually with me in my heart.

CONTENTS

Acknowledgments

I want to thank God for holding my hand and placing me among the most amazing people who inspired me with their talent and knowledge. I wish to thank my family for being at my side every step of the way, especially my children, Sandie and Devon.

To all my friends who have spoken encouraging words and been there for me, I want to say thank you because there were days when you pulled me through, and I will never forget you. Again, thank you.

Mother's Prayer for Her Family

Oh, gracious and mighty God, I come, Lord, lifting you up and giving you the glory and honor. I thank you for your continuous blessing repeatedly and for allowing me to see another day. Lord, you are gracious just for being there with me through all my trials and tribulations, keeping me safe from danger and harm, and directing my path. You are my light that shines within. Lord, I bow before you and declare that you are my Lord over every area of my life. I surrender myself to you so that you can take full control. Without you, I can do nothing. Lord, I thank you for your mercy and grace, your love and compassion, and for making it possible for me to understand your words. I also pray that you would watch over my family, keep your protecting arms around them, and keep them safe from the hands of their enemies. Provide for all their needs ask you to lead and guide them into your perfect truth and surround them in the shadow of your wings. I ask that you bless my family with your favor and thank you for them, Amen.

~Minister Carolyn Morgan~

Mother's Love

A mother's prayer is a prayer that cannot be duplicated. This prayer comes from the heart and reaches the heart of all who may be around her at the time. She asks that all her children be given grace and mercy to carry out the task that is set before them. Mothers also ask God to place a hedge of protection around their children so if one falls they will have each other to hold. There was a mantle from our father given to our mother. This mantle has now passed to us, her children, to continue the journey leaning and depending on God for everything.

~Artherine Warr~

Mother's Prayer for Her Children

Father, I come giving you the glory, the honor, and the praise, thank you for all you have done and what you are going to do. Lord, I lift my children before you. Lord, you have given them to me, and I thank you. Now, Lord, I offer them back to you, so you can obtain them on what you want them to be. You have kept them and watched over them. Now, throw your arms around them, lead them, and guide them for the rest of their lives. In Jesus' name. Amen

~Minister Shirley Martin~

Praises of Prayer

Prayer is the key to life. Many years ago, my wife and I decided to leave the noise and congestion of Los Angeles. We were seeking tranquility and quietness. At that time, we were both employed in the aircraft industry. Yes, we could have just moved, but God needed to be a part of everything we do in our lives, so we prayed and prayed and waited for God's answer because there was no doubt in our minds that it takes prayer, vision and trusting Gods plan completely to make our dreams become reality. In our society today, people make too many hasty decisions and God is not a part of them at all, so I challenge you to seek God first in everything you do and always remember "First not Last" Presently, we are living our dreams in Wichita, Kansas on a six-and-a-half acre spread where the sun shines on rainy days because we know that God will make a plan for us.

~Rev. Charles Jackson~

Mama pray for me

Where would I be without prayer? And where would you be without prayer?

I do not know the answer, but I know somebody pray for us. I thank God that I came from a family who survived on prayers, and even when I did not understand why my parents prayed so much, my mother would tell me, just live, but I get it now. I understand. "Mother I Got it," and I know why you always said all those words for me, "The Lord will make a way somehow." God is the same from yesterday, today, and forever, and God is still making a way for our family, even now that our parents are gone. Lord, give us strength in our weakness, give us faith where there is fear, help us walk by faith and not by sight, and bless my sister, Alicia, and everyone who has read this book, In Jesus' name.

~Rev. Russell Jackson

Time to Pray

Come on. Let's go to a private place and meditate on the Lord. Let His presence take over us as we lift our hands to the sky. Lord, I adore You. I place no one before You in the morning when I rise. If you are living, it is praying time every morning. It's a new day, so I run to my private place, where You prepare me for the battlefield to rejuvenate my strength. It's like breakfast, the most important and nutritious meal of the day, and it sets the tone. It promotes weight maintenance and weight loss by maintaining blood glucose levels and metabolism. This breakfast is for your body, not your soul. I can say we are spiritual beings, and we have souls, and the nutrient we need is prayer. It is our direct line to God, a communication process that allows us to talk to God. It's personal between you and your God, and guess what? He wants to tell everyone. He is waiting, so come on. Tell Him to forgive your sins, cleanse you, and make you whole. Tell Him about your needs, your cares. Just tell Him, "Thank you."

In the morning, at noon, and late in the evening, pray, "I will follow my Master's orders." Prayer provides the nutrients for our souls. It rejuvenates, strengthens, and encourages us. It gives us the hope, peace, joy, and love that are essential for our lives, and we truly lack these nutrients. When everything around us is caving down on our heads, prayer is the last thing we think about, or we do not even think about it at all. Bible classes should be crowded, churches should overflow—north, south, east, and west—and every voice all over should ask, "What must I do to be saved?" because no man knows the hour or the time, and because we don't know, we close our eyes when our eyes should be open because death is like a thief in the night.

Mothers and fathers, pray for your children. Lay your children before God because He knows what to do. Our children are getting lost in a world that takes and takes until there is nothing left. Oh, but if parents get on their knees and call out His name, if wife and husband pray for each other, although they are different, they should come together as one because you all are one in His sight. Grandmothers and grandfathers, pray for your grandchildren. Sisters and brothers, pray for each other. Neighbors, pray for neighbors, and all of us, pray for love and world peace. Please. Time is not on our side, so it's time to pray. Take the time and look around. Tell me what you see. Yes, it's time to get on your knees.

Preface

There is nothing more important in your life than having a relationship with God. Some may feel differently, and that's okay because we are individuals, and that alone will lead to questions. Prayer is not something that just appeared. Prayer existed before you and me. Despite some disbelief or uncertainty about prayer, Abraham practiced it. All the prophets prayed, and of course, Jesus Christ himself prayed. Therefore, this is confirmation that prayer works.

Some of you have said that prayer does work, that prayer does change things, that God does hear your prayers. For you, first, I challenge you to start praying to be embraced in a relationship like no other. I am a product of what prayer can do, coming from a little two-bedroom house with one bathroom, only one parent working, and ten other siblings—a house where prayers were heard from the front to the back, where prayer was transforming our lives. Thank God for the movement of prayer. If God has done anything for you, say amen.

1

Mama's House

I grew up with ten other siblings in a little two-bedroom house on a dusty road in a small town called New Roads, thirty miles from Baton Rouge, where a train track divided one side of the town from the other. For our family, prayer was the most important thing while we lived here on Earth. Our parents prayed every morning, noon, and evening, calling on the Lord, who provided for us, protected us, and guided us throughout our lives and still does today. Yes, we survived on prayer. The faded areas on the rug were where their knees were pressed against the floor on the side of the bed, and the wall cracked from the strength of their voices as my parents cried out, "Lord, take care of our children!"

We knew God was the only one taking care of us. It was no secret. We depended on God. Being the youngest child in that home, I laid my head between my mother and father every night, and when my father went to work at night, he would always bring me back a sandwich that he had taken for lunch. What was special about the sandwich was that the bread would always be stuck to the meat with mayonnaise and mustard. What a treat!

The love our parents had for us is unforgettable, and no, we didn't have a lot of money. No, we didn't have a closet full of clothes nor a refrigerator full of food, but what we did have had come from love. I watched my father walk everywhere he needed to go, but it seemed okay.

Maybe he needed more quiet quality time to talk to the Lord because we never missed a meal. We had a roof over our heads and clothes on our backs. My daddy was the best daddy ever.

Sometimes I would see him crying, and he would say, "Baba, it's going to be all right."

I would comb his hair and tell him, "I love you," and he would give me a nickel, and somehow I would put that nickel back in his pocket.

I was not blind, and as a child, I knew God saw his tears and heard his cry because he talked to God all day long. The God my parents served moved mountains, and it was known that no one could pray or sing like my daddy. He would whistle as he walked down the road "What a Friend We Have in Jesus." He was a gifted man and a caring person. He would call every last one of us "baba." His love was never in doubt, and he loved the Lord especially. His nickname was "nappy chin." I did know why—because his hair was good.

My parents never complained. They told God everything. We got new clothes for Christmas and Easter. God was so good. Despite life's hiccups and messes as well as setbacks my parents may have had, the Lord's Prayer was the first thing I had heard and learned. Our parents were humble and quiet. I know tongues and teeth fall out, but I never heard them argue. I only saw their love. They were as one. My mother was also the one to pray first.

She would start by saying, "Our Father who art in heaven, hallowed be Thy name. Thy kingdom come, Thy will be done on Earth as it is in heaven. Give us this day our daily bread and forgive us our trespasses as we forgive those who trespass against us, and lead us not into temptation but deliver us from evil, for Thine is the kingdom and the power and the glory for ever and ever. Here I am again, your faithful servant."

The words would just flow out of her mouth nonstop, and I am sure she thought about the way God carried her from the moment her mother had left her playing outside in the yard and was never seen again, praising Him and thanking Him for fighting her battles, for giving her the strength to endure, for just keeping His promises for that moment.

Coming from a home where prayer resided, I know truly for myself, without a doubt, that I must pray because God is the one who puts food on my table and the one who puts clothes on my back. I couldn't see Him, but I knew He was there. Now, at fifty-six, looking back and thinking, I know all my parents' prayers stored up in God's kingdom were for us, and today we are still living on their prayers. Eleven children lived in that two-bedroom house. Come on, you can say it—"That can't be"—and I can say, "Yes, that was real, and each one of us has his or her own stories about our parents and their relationship with God." So right now, you are "hanging" with me, the baby in the family, and I can tell you that two bedrooms became three because that is the kind of God we serve—a giving God.

Growing up, I had a close friend. We would talk all the time. Maybe he was sweet on me, I don't know, but he would ask me, "Why did your mother have so many children? She has to buy a lot of food."

I would say, "My mama prays! I could see it and hear it."

His last words would always be "My family goes to church. I never see it or hear it. Maybe *some* people need to pray."

As kids, we hear things and shake them off sometimes, but if he was still living today, I would "pop him upside the head" because he was all in my parents' business. I have learned that life can bring situations, and you just have to accept them, good or bad, because most of the time, you can't change anything. You just have to wait on God.

As a child, I had always wanted to be a scientist. I would catch insects, watch their behavior, and try to analyze why they did this or that, but I also studied my mother. I would watch her and the way she carried herself and the way she was content in her situation. She would tell me to ask God to teach me to be still so I can see Him moving in my life, so now that's my prayer: "Lord, keep me still, for I am quick to do things my way." So now I ask God to keep me still because I find myself tossing and turning about earthly things. "Lord, keep me still so that I can be like You and see You moving in my life."

My siblings and I are all walking in our parents' shoes, and God has given all of us different instructions. I have two brothers who are pastors, two sisters who are ministers, one brother who is a minister of music, and one brother who is a deacon, and the remaining five are messengers of the Lord. Being raised in a home where prayer was heard in every direction throughout the day, evening, and night, I had no doubt that

God was in the center of it all. Prayer moves mountains. Prayer changes things. We are a living testimony, and the praying never stopped. I have siblings whom I call praying warriors: Rev. Russell Jackson, Rev. Charles Jackson, Minister Shirley Martin, and Minister Carolyn Morgan. If you are wearing a hat, they can pray it off your head. I'm not clowning.

There are times we would get together and talk about our parents, how they prayed all day and it didn't matter who was around. Nothing could interfere with those times you could hear them praying. Their prayers would be so long, but now I understand, and sometimes I smile to myself, thinking, *Look how far God has brought us. Thank You. Thank You for our parents.* The pillow talks we had were wonderful and somewhat magical, the way God would show up when they didn't have money or food to put on the table.

Mama would say to me, "I watch my God move in our lives, in my life, child."

We had nothing, and what we did have was not taken for granted. What I would give to wake up and smell the aroma of brewing coffee in her kitchen as she made flapjack pancakes for breakfast with the syrup in the yellow can! Oh, in the morning, when songbirds sing their first songs and roosters say cock-a-doodle-doo, it is a new day, a day never seen before. My parents would ease themselves into their hushed space and meditate on the Lord, letting His presence overtake them, and I can imagine them lifting their hands to the sky, saying, "Lord, we adore You. We place no one before You in the morning when we rise." Without a doubt, I know my mother told the Lord, "Thank You for watching over us all night. Thank You," words that penetrated deep down in her heart. She was just thankful.

We had the best times ever in Mama's house, which was full of laughter and joy, and yet so many people think money is the answer. *God* is the answer, and we had all we needed. Holiday cheer—oh, what a Christmas! The fragrance from Mama's fruit bowl was splendid— apples and oranges. Her homemade cakes that sat on her table—five-layer banana, coconut, pineapple. You dream it, she could bake it. We also had all kinds of homemade food from family members. Life was good at Mama's house. Mama's house was blessed.

2

The Storm

As a young child, I would always compare the weather to life because there was something about a sunny day. Everyone would come out, including the cats and dogs, but now I really know that life is like the weather. We have cloudy, rainy, foggy, sunny, and windy days, but please don't forget the stormy ones. Every day, when I get up, I check the weather so I can prepare in case I need my umbrella or if I need to leave early for work, but there's no way to check the weather in our daily lives, so there is no other way to prepare but with prayer because life is unpredictable.

On February 15, 1970, a storm came up with winds of a hundred miles per hour that shattered our windows and jiggled the doors on our home. I still remember it like it was yesterday. It was seven o'clock in the morning on Monday, and my Mama was combing my hair for school. Every light was on in the house.

Everyone was getting ready slowly because there was only one bathroom, and Mama was yelling, "Get ready for school! The bus with be here soon!"

While all that was going on, I was crying to have two ponytails rather than one. We heard the phone ring and wondered why.

My mama answered the phone and said, "Hello."

It was my father's close friend whom he rode to work with. She held the phone, just listening. She never said a word. Then she just put the phone down. There was a silent pause as she looked for the words to say to her children.

"Daddy just got killed at work."

The news traveled near and far that Louis had been killed that morning, and the doors were opening and closing all day nonstop. That morning, Mama could not get the house clean enough. People were everywhere. My eldest sister (Annie Bell) kept things in order. Thank you, Annie Bell. You always have been the decorator of the family.

Our lives changed forever that morning. My mama did not receive any notice, any memo. She could not hit rewind on the tape recorder. The storm, the wind, took her breath away. The heavy rains washed away her future dreams with my daddy. Thunder and lightning scattered her mind and thoughts. It all happened in the blink of an eye. The loss of our daddy was sad, but Mama's relationship with God was like no other. The word on the street was "How's she going to take care of all the children?" They did not know she had God on her side.

The morning of my daddy's funeral, the sun was bright, and the wind was still as we stepped into Verrette's Pointe Coupee funeral limousine. There was not much talking, but I felt like this day was final and that the ride was not long at all. As the driver was pulling up, all you could see were cars of all colors and makes. It was my daddy's homegoing. When we entered the church, there was no standing room. There was a slate blue casket in front of the altar, surrounded by flowers, and the choir was singing as we were being seated, with the tears running down our faces. My elder brother LJ stood at the casket. No one could get him to sit down, but he also knew that this was final. At the end of the service, we eleven children surrounded Daddy's casket as the choir sang "I Am Going Up Yonder to Be with My Lord."

I heard my sister TT say, "We won't see Daddy anymore," and my brother Gee was staring up at the sky, while Annie Mae was drenched in tears.

We were all twisted and bent up inside but not broken. My mama stood like the tree planted by the river. God kept His promises. God became her husband. She never married again. God supplied all our needs. He talked and walked with my mama. Yes, He answered all her prayers. People said that eleven children's daddy was gone and that there was no way they would be all right, that there were too many children, but God wrapped His arms around us and covered us like an eagle. Mama was never in a courthouse. She never went to the jailhouse. She never needed a lawyer. She went to eleven graduations, eight weddings, and innumerable events related to her children and truly enjoyed her children's singing and their musical gifts. We are the Jacksons, and we are all here today.

As I go back down memory lane and think about the way my mama and daddy were, I realize they knew the key to life *was* God and *is* God, no matter what came their way. They knew when they passed through the water, God would be with them. They knew when they passed through the river, they would not be swept away. They knew if they walked through the fire, they would not be burned because Isaiah 43:2 says so. My parents kept their eyes on God because no man knows what day the Lord is coming. I can say my mother was prepared.

There is an old saying: "Actions speak louder than words." Her relationship with God carried her through, and she knew He was with her. When I say all I heard was praying growing up, this is so real, and her praying never ceased. I felt like she had a direct line to God, and her wisdom and knowledge about God were remarkable. I had never heard my mama ask God, "Where are You?" There's something about an intimate relationship. She knew God was right there and that God would come through, and that was a fact.

Every storm is different. Some have extremely high winds or heavy rain and hail, but it doesn't matter. The unexpected occurs. Storms are just a part of life, and if you are not equipped for them, they can disrupt your life in a flash. Certain storms in life, we bring upon ourselves, storms that could have been avoided, but when you face storms, they strengthen and advance you. No matter who you are, you are either coming out of a storm, in a storm, or heading for a storm. Where you are really doesn't matter. What matters is the kind of relationship you have with God (Psalm 91):

> Whosoever dwells in the shelter of the highest will rest
> in the shadow of the Almighty. I will say of the Lord,

"He is my refuge and my fortress, my God, in whom I trust." Surely, He will save you from the fowler's snare and from the deadly pestilence. He will cover you with His feathers, and under His wings, you will find refuge. His faithfulness will be your shield and rampart. You will not fear the terror of night nor the arrow that flies by day nor the pestilence that stalks in the darkness nor the plague that destroys at midday. A thousand may fall at your side, ten thousand at your right hand, but it will not come near you. You will only observe with your eyes and see the punishment of the wicked. If you say, "The Lord is my refuge," and you make the highest your dwelling, no harm will overtake you. No disaster will come near your tent. For He will command His angels concerning you to guard you in all your ways. They will lift you up in their hands so that you will not strike your foot against the stone. You will tread on the lion and cobra. You will trample the great lion and the serpent. "Because he loves me," says the Lord, "I will rescue him. I will protect him, for he acknowledges my name. He will call on me, and I will answer him. I will be with him in trouble. I will deliver him and honor him. With long life, I will satisfy him and show him my salvation."

3

The Storm Has Passed

The rain was gone, the sun was shining, and the storm had passed. Things were different after my daddy's funeral. We had trouble adjusting and moments of crying and not understanding, but time heals all things. My mama became our father also, so now she was everything, and yes, there was no doubt people were wondering how we were going to make it and questioning how she was going to raise five boys without a father, saying, "Those boys won't be nothing." I am sure they were floored when they realized those Jackson boys were staying at home. They never got into any trouble, and they were very respectful, as her daughters were too.

I must say Mama was made from a very tough material. Every word from her mouth was firm with a splash of kindness, and her prayer was powerful. "God, I am calling on You. Protect my children. Cover my children. Lead my children. Never leave them because You are their father. You know everything about them, their weaknesses and their strengths. Put them on Your path so that they won't stray." Oh, she knew how to call Jesus's name. "Give my children Your mind and Your heart so they can conquer this world instead of the world conquering them." Then she would be silent for a moment, with her eyes closed, and it was all for her children. We were always first. Her life revolved around us, and this continued until God took her home.

Mama was content, and we never wondered what we were going to eat—breakfast in the morning, *hot* lunch, and dinner on time. My mama could cook, and everything she touched was good. As time passed, the crowded house started to feel some changes—growth and other good things. Mama later was able to get another room added to the house—Yes, Lord—which gave us a little more room, and I have to say, "Thank you, Lord, for a hot water heater, a television, and a new sofa" because that sofa we had was gold and made from some type of leather. When I think about the sofa, I only recall my legs sticking to it and sweating. There were a lot of changes, all good ones, although we never had a garden anymore.

My brother Russell, "Crip," would always tell Mama, "Don't worry, Mama. I will continue with the garden," which never happened.

Mama would say it was all right, and that was because he was a Mama's boy. To be honest, all her boys were Mama's boys. They were very close, but it was such a joy to see my brother Buck wash his special shirts or pants, hang them on the clothesline to dry, and go back later to get them, and they would be gone. One of my other brothers would be wearing his clothes. My brothers were somewhat different. Crip would beat Mama's pots most of the day. He was an outstanding self-taught drummer. Point was a self-taught lead and bass guitar and keyboard player, all from ear. It was awesome. LJ was the overseer of everything, his and ours, Gee was the peacemaker, and Buck was the quiet one. Mama's girls were Annie Bell and Shirley, the basketball players, Annie Mae, the cry baby, TT, the smart one, Carolyn Boo, the fashion girl, and Blackie, the different one.

God blessed Mama with the strength and courage to endure whatever came our way. We never heard, "I am tired," or even saw her get displeased. She would say, "God will make a way somehow." We never saw her cry. She always had a smile on her face, and she loved to laugh.

One evening, about six o'clock, we were all sitting around in the house. We were going to have baked fish that night for dinner, so Mama got the catfish out of the refrigerator. The fish needed to be cleaned, so she placed it on the table to clean it, but then she started doing something else. My daddy had a habit, before he passed away, of bringing home stray animals, so we had a dog and a yellow-and-white cat. Anyway, that evening, the cat got in the house somehow without anyone noticing him. Later, when Mama returned to the kitchen, she didn't see the fish on the table, so she thought someone had put it back in the refrigerator, but when she looked in the refrigerator, it wasn't in there.

Mama yelled out, "Where is the fish I put on the table?"

We all said, "What fish? We didn't see any fish."

She replied that someone had taken the fish we were going to have for dinner off the table, and so we all started looking for the stolen fish. We looked everywhere in the kitchen, and then we started looking in the bedroom—but still no fish. Then Annie Mae looked under the back bed and saw the cat under the bed, eating the fish. Mama was upset, and so were we because now we didn't know what we were going to have for dinner. Everything was frozen, and the cat had eaten our dinner.

Suddenly, Mama started laughing and said, "I never seen nothing like this before. The cat took the fish. This is something else."

Then thanks to the cat, she took out frozen ground beef that was harder than a brick. The cat died later that year, and Daddy's dog got hit by the milkman in front of the house.

Every evening, around six o'clock, Mama would get her chair and a towel to fan the mosquitoes off her while she sat on the porch, and we would also go and sit on the porch. Mama would always tell us to stick together and that it didn't matter how we fussed and got mad. At the end of the day, we are all sisters and brothers, and we must love one another and stick together, and these words were repeated on her dying bed. That was the most important thing of all.

4

Sunday

"Wake up. Get dressed. Get your Bible. Let's go to church."

Every Sunday we would start early—breakfast waiting, lunch cooking, clothes freshly ironed. Mount Era Baptist Church was our second home: Sunday school, speaking meeting, prayer meeting, church services, everything. I felt like my mama was a part of every organization in the church, and as time passed, she became the mother of the church before God called her home. We joined the choir, and Jaywalker was our musician. My brother Russell was a killer on the drum, a great singer off the chain. Later, my brother Point showed up to play the keyboard and lead and bass guitar. It made us scream. Our choir was known and invited everywhere. You had to be there to experience the Spirit.

"Let the church say amen!"

The choir would march in, wearing their burgundy and gray robes, swaying from side to side, and singing, "Step by step, we'll make this journey, even though our way seems hard. Step by step, we'll make this journey, but we must put our trust in God."

God would show up and turn the whole church service around because we were making this journey. Yes, God was moving through all our tears, hurts, and disappointment. Through all the "amens" and "hallelujahs," a scripture was being read (Matthew 9:20–22):

And behold, a woman who was diseased with an issue
of blood for twelve years came behind Him and touched
the hem of His garment, for she said within herself, "If I
may but touch His garment, I shall be whole." But Jesus
turned about, and then He saw her. He said, "Daughter,
be of good comfort. Your faith has made you whole."
And the woman was made whole from that hour.

Following the scripture, there was prayer, the song "I Need Thee,"
two selections, and a solo—"This morning, when I rise, serving the
Lord before the pastor because He lives."

Then Reverend Wright would stand and say, "Isn't God all right?
The scripture been read, the prayer been prayed. I will be preaching
from Matthew 9:20–22. Amen."

He used for the title "Crazy Faith," faith that caused God to stop
and say, "Go, my child. Your faith has healed you" or "Go, my child, and
be blessed." He spoke about the lady who had a condition called issues of
the blood, which lasted for a long time and caused frustration because
she had gone from one physician to another, seeking help, and now she
had no more money, but the condition still existed. He said one day she
had heard about Jesus, and being desperate for a miracle, she came up
behind Him in the crowd and embraced His cloak. "Nevertheless, if I
can just embrace His garment, I will be restored" (Mark 5:27–28). As
soon as she touched Jesus, her bleeding stopped, and she was healed.
Here we go again. Faith appears instantly once more, believing in
something that has not been, though it already is a reality.

He said, "Sometimes, sisters and brothers, let's be real. We pray for
healing, and perhaps you are close to God, but uncertainty is there also.
Faith and trust work in one accord. They can't be separated. With all
the advanced medical technology and treatment, we are living longer,
but are we living or just existing? Throughout the Bible, God is the
healer, and He still is healing today. He never changes. I believe this
woman with the issues of the blood had 'crazy faith,' and it made God
pause and say, 'Who touched me?' Can you imagine what was going
through her mind as she left the temple, shouting, breathing hard,

'Thank you, Lord! I am healed'? Yeah, I come to tell you if you need to be healed, God is here. God is healing His people every day, and perhaps you are one of His children who forgot to say thank you. This is the time to say thank you and tell someone about what He done for you—how He healed you, how He stood by your side and never left you, how He kept His promises. Stay at His feet until He heals you."

Everyone was out of their seats, clapping, heads moving side to side—nothing but a Holy Ghost party. The door of the church was open. "There is a train that is coming. You don't need no ticket. Just get on board." Oh, what a time we had when all God's children got together!

On our way back home, we talked about church, and when we got home, we undressed and continued talking about church. To be honest, we talked about church all week long until the next Sunday. This was normal for the Jackson family. Oh, how we love Jesus because He first loved us! Oh, but "when Sunday comes," the songwriter says, "my trouble's gone. As soon as it gets there, I'll have a new song. When Sunday comes, I won't have to cry no more. Jesus will soothe my troubled mind and all my heartaches. Every burden, all my misery, all my crying, every trial, every tribulation will be left behind when Sunday comes." I have to say that songwriter must have gotten to walk in our shoes because on Sunday, everything was left behind. There was just something about a Sunday at Mama's house. You were not going to miss church, and if you were sick, you were going to get well at church.

We thank God for our parents. We thank God for that two-bedroom house where Mama and Daddy lay before God, not sometimes but all the time, crying out for their eleven children, where their prayer took root in our hearts and grew.

Psalm 1 says, "Blessed is the man who walks not in the counsel of the ungodly nor stands in the way of the sinner nor sits in the seat of the scornful. But his delight is in the law of the Lord, and in His law does he meditate day and night. And he shall be like a tree planted by the river of water that brings forth his fruit in his season. His leaf also shall not wither, and whatsoever he does shall prosper."

5

Confident in God

God's name would chime throughout the house with praises. He was the one who made a way out of no way and provided for our needs. My parents' commitment to God brought about confidence and boldness that has no end and faith that would withstand any storm. Every morning, rain or shine, they got up and thanked the Lord for another day by praying. My parents were confident in God and never wavered. No matter how things looked, they stood on God's words. After my daddy had passed away, my mama took the mantle and showed no sign of fear. She walked in Daddy's shoes like she had done it before. My mama stood tall with confidence and assurance that God was on her side, and there was nothing else she needed.

Despite what may have been said, my mama excelled. Her daily walk with God continued as normal, the smile on her face remained as we embarked on another chapter of our lives, and she never complained. She was always positive, saying, "God's got this."

There have been many times when complications occurred in my life, and I would pray and give God my problems, and before the day was over, I had it back again and a restful night to add to it. How many of us have done this? I know I am not the only one, but perhaps we have not built up enough confidence in God, or maybe we stress about it to cause God to fix it faster. Whatever the reason, it does not reflect what God deserves. Confidence in God means truly not worrying at all, giving it all to God our Father, and resting in Him completely, knowing God's got us. This is what comes from commitment. This commitment doesn't come from praying *sometimes*, reading the Bible *sometimes*, or just doing everything related to God *sometimes*. Your confidence in God increases with time with Him—no time, no confidence; little time, little confidence. Fear and doubt are just around the corner when you have no confidence.

I could hear my mama on the phone giving someone advice: "Why are you burdened? Just give it to God. It's so easy. Trust God." She would make it sound so simple, but she was really trying to say, "Go to sleep. Rest. You can't do nothing. God's got this."

But the question is can you go to sleep and truly rest in God? Here's a little information for those who can't go to sleep in God. Sure, you can try sleep aid medications, and they will help you close your eyes, but the situation will still be the same if you are looking for the answers in the wrong place. I pray that the medication works so you won't wake up with bags under your eyes because sometimes makeup can't cover it, and yes, there are side effects from not resting in God. Let me tell you, you don't need additional stress because stress is connected to hypertension, heart attack, and stroke. I can't say that enough. Information or education is power. It's what you do with it. You can set it on the shelf, or you can use it.

One early morning I received a text message from an old friend laying all her troubles on me, so when I finished reading the message, I said to myself, *This is serious. I hope she is praying.* So I texted her back, and I asked her, "Have you been praying on this?"

She replied, "No, girl. That is why I am texting you—because you pray all the time, and I don't pray. I was not raised the way you were."

I thought, *She talks about God's goodness and mercy, but she doesn't pray. Maybe she doesn't know how to pray.* At that moment, I realized I needed to call her and talk to her. Sometimes we just need a little guidance because we all fall short. To make a long story short, she is now active in church and her daily walk with God, seeking all she can learn about her Father, increasing her confidence in Him daily.

It is never too late to increase your confidence in God because we are created *to rest, not stress*. Sometimes I think about how young my mother was when my daddy had passed away, and I never heard her say anything about love, dating, anything related to getting into another relationship, but what she did say was that God loved her and that was all she needed. Her confidence in God moved her fears and doubt. Have you ever met a positive person? My mother did not believe in talking negatively. It had to be positive. Sometimes we would be clowning and say something negative, and there it went. *Why* is that the right thing to do? She was not having any negative talk around her at all.

My mother probably had many setbacks, but they did not turn her around. She only focused on what was straight ahead. My mother was about action. She was never a person to just say something. She meant everything she said. It was going to get done. There were eleven of us with different personalities and dealing with different situations most of the time, and I know she had to stress sometimes, but I don't really know because everything was given to God.

Just the other day, my sister and I were talking about our mother's appearance. Her face had no wrinkles. She had no bags under her eyes. We came to conclusion that she had done a lot of resting and that she had died without a wrinkle and bags under her eyes. I must say if you are a confident woman, the devil will have a hard time with you because confident women are not going to lie back, step back, turn back. A confident woman stands, and there is no breaking. She sits at the Master's feet, covering her family and her blessings. Devil, you are not taking anything from me. You have done enough. A confident woman is always prepared and ready and knowing that the Lord, and his mighty power, is on her side.

Put on the full armor of God so that you can take your stand against the devil's schemes, for our struggle is not against flesh and blood but against the ruler, against the authorities, against the power of the dark world, and against the evil spiritual forces in the heavenly realm.

Therefore, put on the full armor of God so that when
the day of evil comes, you may be able to stand your
ground. After you have done everything to stand, stand
firm then, with the belt of truth buckled around your
waist, with the breastplate of righteousness in place,
and with your feet fitted with the readiness that comes
from the gospel of peace. In addition to all this, take up
the shield of faith, with which you can extinguish all
the flaming arrows of the evil one. Take the helmet of
salvation and the sword of the Spirit, which is the word
of God, and pray in the Spirit on all occasions with
all kinds of prayers and requests. With this in mind,
be alert and always keep on praying for all the Lord's
people. (Ephesians 6:10–18)

I pray that every woman becomes a confident woman in spite of
setbacks, fear, doubt, whatever it is because it is long overdue. It is time
to say no to the devil, and the time is *now*.

6

The Pink Recliner

As time passed, age revealed itself, and Mama changed in some ways, but prayer was still first in her life. In Mama's den, on the left side, right in front of the window, sat a recliner in multiple shades of pink that sat high, with many buttons on the remote that she never used. This pink recliner had stolen her heart. Perhaps it was the color.

Every morning she would wake up and lie quietly in her bed without a sound. Then out of nowhere, you could hear mumbling that lasted for a long time, and not knowing she had an audience, she would start singing, "At the cross, where I first saw the light and the burden of my heart rolled away, it was here by faith I received my sight, and now I am happy all day," and would repeat that verse over and over.

Suddenly, after she fell silent, you could hear as she moved around in her room, getting ready to make her grand entry down the stairs to her pink recliner, in which no one could sit but her. She would walk gracefully to the back door to admire her daughter's home and smile.

Then she would turn to the left and say, "Finally, my dwelling place, my recliner."

You could see the joy on her face as she sat in the chair, and later, her eyes would close unhurriedly, and she would begin to pray to the Lord. This would go on throughout the day and after each meal until midnight, bedtime. Then her routine would resume the next day. Age or sickness or any unexpected situation never prevented her from giving God what only God deserves. I can't explain the relationship my mama had with God, and I am not going to try. You just had to be there.

It's ironic that we could never sit in the chair. She would say, "Don't sit in my chair," and if she had left to do something, her first words when she came back were "Get out of my chair."

One early sunny morning, while we were in the kitchen, cooking breakfast, I asked her, "Mama, do you love your recliner?"

She replied, "Yes, it's my chair," like someone wanted her chair. "Yes, I love my chair. It's my praying chair. This chair is my last dwelling place. My work here is done." She was happy in that chair and would clap her hands and say, "It's all right. I am going home."

My response was "You are already home, Mama," but I knew she was referring to her heavenly home.

Still, she never stopped praying for us. She never stopped calling out our names one by one, asking the Lord to take care of her children. Although all her children were already grown, we were still her babies, and parents never stop praying for their children.

The pink recliner is now a part of the family. It's no longer a piece of furniture. It's a part of our hearts, and it still looks new. You would think after all the years she sat in that chair, it would be ready for the trash, but every button still works, and the color has not faded. In 2015, when my mama's health was failing, she was sitting in her pink recliner at about 5:00 p.m. when she had to be rushed to the hospital. A week later, she answered God's call: "Come home, my child, and rest." What a day. It was her day, her homegoing, a day she had talked about for a very long time. Her preparation was complete.

Driving to Mama's house that day seemed to take a long time, or maybe it was only me. My sister and I went back down memory lane. I felt it would help us mentally, reliving the good old days, days that put smiles on our faces and gave us memories that would last forever, including memories of Mama in her pink recliner.

As we got closer to Mama's house, my sister asked, "We are not bringing Mama home?"

I said, "No. She went to her heavenly home."

When we drove up to the house, we both jumped out of the car to get inside, to go to the chair. That was strange. We were both rushing into the house to sit in the chair, and we could see my mama there, saying, "Get out of my chair."

I felt such emptiness inside. Both Mama and Daddy were gone. I had some time to spend sitting in Mama's pink recliner on the morning of her homegoing, and it felt good. I played with all the buttons. The chair is amazing. It swivels and lifts. It was Mama's special recliner, and its pink color represented her compassion, nurturing nature, and unconditional love. Mama's special "dwelling place" was where she had fought and prayed for her family and stood like a tree planted by the river that brings forth luscious fruit each season without fail. Its leaves shall never wither, and all it does shall prosper.

Oh, how I wish she was still sitting in the pink recliner! I wish I could see her eyes closing and her mouth moving and her smiling face just one more time. It has been three years since Mama went home, and her pink recliner still sits in front of the window, where the sun rises and sets and the wind and rain beat against the window. This is a special chair. It's Mama chair.

7

Blessing

Prayer is the greatest blessing of all. As children of God, this is the way we communicate with our Father and the way He blesses us through our prayers. Phenomenal things can happen when you give Him what He is due, which many think is difficult to do when every blessing that God has given us is visible. So when your eyes open in the morning and you have your right mind and your arms and legs are moving, that is a blessing that should motivate you to pray.

Many years ago, I took care of a client who had an accident that had left him paralyzed. We had many conversations, and one day he asked me, "Do you believe in God?"

I replied, "Yes."

He began to ask me why God had let this happen to him. "Now I can't do anything for myself."

I replied, "I don't know why, but only God knows why, and sometimes terrible things happen to the best of us, but it doesn't mean God doesn't love you."

What was so shocking to me was that he had never realized that he could have died in that accident and that it was a blessing he had survived, but he was wondering why when he could have been praying to tell God, "Thank you."

Sometimes I believe grace and mercy are misunderstood because prayer would be the lead runner, not the last runner. God is the Creator and Master of blessing, but somehow things become confused, and we put "I" first when it should be God. We think the things we own are ours, so let's get this straight right now. You don't own anything. You are borrowing. Get this too. When you leave this earth, there are no moving trucks following the hearse.

Three years ago, my sister phoned to tell me that our mother was in the hospital. Mama was ninety-nine years old but truly full of life and still making jokes. She would always say, "I am going home to see my Creator." I have never met a woman like her. She is my role model.

I left work that day and headed home, and it was so amazing, the way my mind was going everywhere. I had this feeling that just did not want to leave me. Tears began to stream down my face as I asked God to drive me home and to give me the strength to endure what was before me. The tables had turned, and now someone had to hold my hand to comfort me and pray for me. My mama's last days were good. She understood that there was nothing the doctors could do for her but keep her comfortable. Both her kidneys had failed, and I will never forget that right after the doctors had told her about her condition, she called my sister to tell her with a smile on her face. She appeared "happy," while we were dying inside.

Later, we gathered around her bed to pray for her, and she began to pray for us, thanking God for her children, asking Him to wrap His arms around us and keep her children together. The prayer was so powerful, the nurses came down and joined us where we were gathered round, listening to our mother. She thanked God for her many blessings. It was like the doors of heaven had opened up as she thanked Him for her ninety-nine years. She asked Him to honor all her prayers and that her children would be content because she was leaving them in His hands, and she knew He would keep His promises. I never thought I would be part of such an amazing and heart-moving blessing. My mother continued to pray for her children, realizing that we were going to need the strength to carry on because she was going to the place where the streets of the city were made of gold as pure as transparent glass.

She was contented and ready, and her last breath left joy on her face as we told her softly, "Mama, it's okay. We will see you someday, and kiss Daddy for us. We love you. Bye-bye."

Tears of sorrow turned into tears of joy. This lady was truly remarkable, and she carried us through even while on her deathbed. God's blessing is breathtaking. There is no one like God. You can look high and low, but you won't find anybody like Him. I might not know everything, but this, I do know. He is the only one. We had started to see a change in her condition on March 11, but it did not stop her. She talked to all her grandchildren that day, telling each one of them to take care of themselves and pray.

In my mind, I can hear her singing, "There is a leak in this old building, and my soul has got to move. My soul has got to move. Ooh, my soul has got to move. There is a leak in this old building, and my soul has got to move. I've got another building, a building not made by man's hands." It was truly a blessing to have had a mother who influenced our lives through her walk with God, and the blessings that she had received from God also blessed us.

> Blessed are the poor in spirit. Blessed are those who mourn. Blessed are those who are persecuted for righteousness's sake. Blessed are you when others revile you and persecute you. (Matthew 5:3–4)

> Blessed rather are those who hear the word of God and keep it. (Luke 11:28)

Thank You, Lord, for blessing us. God's blessing is so amazing. Even if you don't say thank you, His blessing brings about excitement, a feeling you never thought you had. The twist about blessings is that you can be blessed in many ways. There are times when something happens unexpectedly in our lives, and we think it is terrible, but it turns out to be the best thing ever. That is God working in your favor. We wake up in the morning free from pain, living in a home we have dreamed of, our family well, our children good, wearing the best of clothes and working. We are surrounded with blessings. God is great, and He blesses the just and the unjust. So why the downfall when it relates to worship and praising God, giving God what He deserves? Why the question of whether there is a God? Why is there so much doubt?

Every so often, I fly to Chicago. I get so happy making plans on what I am going to do with my son while I am there, and this is truly a blessing, but at the same time, I am also praying, asking God to protect me, to guide the plane, to take me to Chicago, and to bring me back home safely. All this is going on before I get on the plane, but once I am on the plane, my prayer is tripled because I know the devil travels to and from places, and he does not care about me at all.

So what I am trying to say is God blesses us, but are these blessings taken for granted? Are you covering your blessings? So many have been blessed, and then the blessing no longing exists. Somewhere in the excitement, they fail to realize that it is blessing, and it should not be taken for granted. It needs to be covered by prayer and thanking God daily. Yes, God blesses us sometimes, and the devil takes it, steals it, and destroys it, all because some believe that once you receive a blessing, "that's it."

I know there are people who do pray and yet don't say anything about God's goodness. They think it's all them. It's just like driving your car without car insurance. You are taking a chance. Today we are living in a "take a chance" world. Yes, I said it. You get up and get ready for work, get in your nice car, start it, put it in drive, and go. You never think, *I need to pray and ask God to protect me in this car*, knowing you drive by wrecks on the highway, somewhat quiet often. You still don't get it.

A long time ago, we purchased a car, a sweet blue Honda Accord with a sun roof. We were so happy, and it felt good. Our first new car—who would have known? Two weeks later, we had an accident—car totaled, gone, just like that. Thanks, God. His grace had saved us because we did not deserve it, because to pray while in the car was the last thing on our minds, young and free. "Living on the edge" is what I call it—not good.

I pray you are praying and giving God what God deserves. The shield is God and always will be God. We can't hide from anything. There is no running, and money does not have any power when it comes to God's work.

Parent, you got up this morning, did you tell the Lord thank you for this day? Did you thank God for watching your family all night long and for keeping a roof over your family's heads? Parent, when you got up this morning, did you lay your children before God, asking God to lead and guide your children and protect them from harm? Parent, when you got up this morning, did you thank God for everything God has done and what God is going to do? Taking the time to pray and to thank God is the easiest thing of all, but some do not believe this. Is it somewhat placed on the "to-do list"?

I am going to let you in on a little secret. If you are breathing with no difficulties, that is a blessing because there is someone this very morning having problems with breathing. That is a reason to take the time to say thank you to God. If you woke up this morning, I know you need to say thank you to God, or maybe you need to read the newspaper or read it on your phone. We are dying every minute of the day, and there are no age limits. Take the time to look around. Tell me what you see.

Four years ago, on Christmas Eve Day, my mother and I were in the kitchen making a cake, the old-fashioned cake, not from Betty Crocker's cake mix or "the box." My mother talked about how we sometimes overlook blessings because they are never thought of until they are not there or they are different. The conversation was linked to the movement of her hand, the uniqueness of the human hand, and her hand no longer being able to grip tightly anymore, and that was a big thing. It is a blessing to be able to grip anything with your hand. Not all blessings are huge. They come in many ways and forms when you are dealing with life itself. I have cared for many stroke patients, and I truly believe they can put a light on blessing.

A year ago, my sister (Annie Mae) became sick, and this unfavorable disease hurriedly affected her daily activities of living. This disease had no care at all. It had signs of a stroke, but it was a stroke. She went back and forth to the doctor, X-rays, and labs, but our praying continued. So many times, I spoke to my sister on the phone, and she would just cry and say, "Oh, how I wish I could do something for myself." Today the unfavorable disease is being treated. She can feed herself. She can walk and dress herself. If you would talk to her this day or on any day, she would tell you how God has blessed her and how easy it is to overlook blessings.

Yes, we get content. It will always be the same mentality, but I'm here to tell you things do change with time. I have many friends who are married, and boy, they can say something, and in the back of my mind, I am saying that is a blessing, especially when you have a good spouse. To have a wife or a husband is a blessing because, girl, I am praying for God to send me the man whom He has chosen for me right now and to please give me a sign so that I would know that this is the "right dude." Say what you want. I am not alone on this one. Everyone wants someone in their life, but the Lord knows the right one. Lord, I don't have time for fussing, going against one another for small things, things that don't matter.

We need to take that time and pray for one another and love one another because one day a change is going to come, and you will miss your spouse and everything about that person. We take so much for granted, and we don't miss anything until it's gone. Our lives are full of blessings, whether or not you see them. When you think your life is a mess, just take a moment, think about what God has done for you, and then look at your blessings and know this too shall pass because nothing lasts forever.

8

I Have Fought a Good Fight, and I Have Finished My Course; I Have Kept the Faith (11 Timothy 4:7)

That early Saturday morning was a still, quiet morning, never seen before. With so many thoughts in our heads and so many memories in our hearts, we stepped back into the reality that we were burying our mama on this day, March 14, 2015. As we gathered at Mama's house, dressed in black, there was food everywhere, and it seemed like a flashback to 1970, when we had buried our father as we were burying our mother now. As we sat in that same living room, waiting for a limousine from the same funeral home, Verrette's Pointe Coupee Funeral Home, the family was five times larger now, with thirty-three grandchildren and fifty-nine great-grandchildren. Mama's grandson, my brother's son, Geroid Jackson, had died the day before her, and it felt somewhat like a dream and that all I needed to do was wake up. This was a trying time for the Jackson family, but God never left us.

The ride to the funeral home seemed to be short, perhaps because my mind was in a foreign place. As we entered the church, heaven's doors opened, the choir sounded like angels, and the sound of the trumpet brought peace to my troubled soul as my mama lay still for all to see in a gleaming white casket with a touch of silver and a variety of

flowers in all colors. She rested in her casket, which was surrounded by flowers from its head to its foot, with more from one end of the church to the other. There was no standing room at all, and there were more people outside than inside. Even though the church was large, it simply was not large enough. This lady had influenced many lives, young and old, and her wisdom and knowledge exceeded all, proving that prayer is the key to living. There was no doubt we were at a celebration. People had come from everywhere. It is so fascinating, the way news travels by word of mouth.

The choir continued to sing, and as God's spirit surrounded the church, it was like Mama wanted us to know she was gone and that it was time to release her: "Let me go. I have so many things to see and do. You mustn't tie yourself down with tears. *Be happy that we had so many good years.*" So I will bless the memories in my heart, for there so are many. The celebration was so wonderful. How could it have been a funeral? It was magnificent, from the second we walked into the church to the last words of the eulogy Pastor Gil Wright gave, but now the time had come for the final viewing, and it was like something had hit us. The tables had turned, the clock stopped, and watery eyes and tears appeared as Mama lay still in her snow-white suit with silver touches around the collar and with diamond-and-pearl earrings, with a matching bracelet and pearls around her neck, made up flawlessly with "Treekie" touch and a white frost mesh linen church hat accented with net trim with a downturn.

As we gathered around her for the very last time, the kisses and "I love yous" never ceased, and we said, "We're going to miss you," "Mama, we will miss you," "She won't sit in her chair anymore," and "Mama, don't leave us, please" as the mortician tried to make his way through the crowd. The benediction was given, the pallbearers were standing ready, and the casket was closed, but when they got to the door of the church, my brother Buck reopened it. He didn't want it closed and told LJ repeatedly that they were closing Mama up. Once he understood, we all got in the limousine and proceeded to Mount Era Baptist Church, "our home." The church was full of people waiting for her arrival, and they sat with her for a few minutes until she was laid to rest.

All our lives, people have come and gone, some for the duration and others just passing through. Throughout this journey, one remained true—*our mother, our friend*—and heaven is expecting you, but before you leave, we want you to know that your memory will live on. You were unique in your own way, always one step ahead of the rest, God's best-kept secret, one He decided to share with the rest. As we all think over times and moments past, we know you prepared us well. We are great women and men because of your words and actions. Sometimes we didn't get it, but now we understand, and everything made a lot of sense. You were there for us when others were not, and we shared a special relationship with you throughout. You were someone we could run to who would listen and dry our tears, although our hearts were heavy, and our eyes wouldn't dry. We have no need to wonder because we are certain you are with our heavenly Father, and we don't want to say goodbye because we will see you again. We will miss you, Mama, dear friend.

I thank God every day for placing me in my parents' lives. Yes, we were poor, like the songwriter said—"I come from a poor family, but the Lord has been good to me." Yes, God has been good to all of us. So as we laid Mama down to rest, a smile came to my face as I thought, *What a warrior of God.*

9

God Is in Control

When you pray, you invite God into your life. You allow Him to move in every situation in your life. God is a God who is out of the box. He will show up, clean up, and straighten up. He is a God who hears all prayers without limitation. As I go back down memory lane, I think about my parents, true servants who were anchored in God's words completely, souls out. My siblings and I talk about our parents' relationship with God all the time. If we didn't know the meaning of commitment, we learned it firsthand at home from the example of our parents' dedication, devotion, loyalty, and faithfulness. Prayer were pray everywhere, inside and outside. *Oh, if that fig tree could talk.* A house that prays together stays together, they say, and we are living testimonies of that.

Some may think prayer is something that you have to schedule in your daily life. If someone were to ask, "Does prayer really work?" my mother would always say, "Try Him. I dare you." My mother would sit in her recliner and testify how she was saved, how, when she was nine, she sat on the bench for a week or more until she had a vision. She sat there daily, waiting for a voice or a vision of the Lord Almighty. Then one day she heard His voice. She explained that it felt "triumphant." Prayer meetings were a time for praying, and the prayers would be long as the members in the church rocked from side to side in response to the prayers. "Instant" was what my mama had called her God. Everywhere He went, there was change. Everything He said was "right now." She watched God do everything He said He would do for her, and if He ever promises you anything, you can be sure it's coming. All her faith was in God. He was her bread when she was hungry and water when she was thirsty, so when you pray with faith, God moves. Faith gets His attention and causes the wall to fall.

Sometimes—yes, sometimes—we pray for special conditions that He is just not going to honor because it is not His will. God moves in your life according to His will. Years ago, my life collapsed without any warning, and everything became disorganized. I tried hard to fix it, but it only got worse. I would have to say it was in God's plan, and I had no control, so you have to know that whatever is in God's plans for you, it will manifest no matter what. I have learned that God is not a God you can pray to and tell the way you want the prayer to be answered, so don't waste your time. He'll answer your prayer in His time and according to His will, so don't try to understand.

God moved me out of my first home—yes, that is what I said—and into an apartment. I had no plans to do that *at all*. However, God had a plan. I stayed in that apartment for eight months, and I am telling you, God would wake me up around 3:00 a.m., and I would pray, read my Bible, and write. This went on for some time, and really, I didn't know what was going on, and I had no control.

One early Monday morning God whispered in my ear and said, "Get up, songbird." I stood up and grabbed my head, and His voice in my mind said, "Start looking for a house today."

I thought, *Okay, I got that*, or, just clowning, *Maybe I need to see a psychiatrist*. My name was still on the house I had left with another person whom I was *not* married to. My credit was all messed up, and I thought, *I have to be crazy*. I got ready for work, got in my car, and went to work, expecting that all this would just vanish, but no. Here we go again. I *cannot* explain it, but I was up the next morning and dressed at five o'clock, and I called in sick that day. I could not wait until daylight came because of the night and the early morning I had endured. Finally, morning came. I had my instructions and was sitting in front of a model home two hours before it opened. At approximately 10:45 a.m., a young man arrived eagerly, all fired up.

He said, "Come in. This is a beautiful morning."

I didn't reply as my eyes were fixed on the price. He began showing me the floor plan, but I told him I wanted something built and ready to move in. We looked at four homes that morning, but the last one touched my heart. *It was talking to me.* Later, while standing in the kitchen, I asked the real-estate agent to call their company's preferred lender, and I gave the lender all my information. In minutes, she informed me that I was approved for the home or that I could get another, more expensive home. The feeling I had was beyond words. I thought, *God is God all by Himself.* I didn't understand what she had said because I had checked my credit score the day before, and it wasn't good, but every day is a new day. God had given me so much. I could never repay Him, but *I can praise Him and tell the world about His goodness and mercy.* The "instant God" was what my mama had called him. Well, I felt like Tony the Tiger: *He is great! My God is great!* You can't get through on this life's journey without God.

There are incalculable closures and deviations. Prayer is the main ingredient. While living here on Earth, we must pray. My parents knew they had to lay a foundation for us through their walk with God because God is the main source we need to survive. There is no other. We learned how to pray, how to seek Him first, and that everything else would be provided and so much more. Being a single parent, I watched prayer take me from an uncertain place to a place called "God's got this." I became my parents. I went back to my old landmark. I knew times change, but God stays the same. Sometimes we think we can do things without help, or the help we are seeking is no help at all. From the promises God makes us, you would think we would just go to our Father who art in heaven the moment trials and tribulations enter our lives, but no. We go everywhere else but God.

Psalm 107:28–30 says, "Then they cried to the Lord in their trouble, and He delivered them from distress. He made the storm be still, and the waves of the sea were hushed. Then they were glad that the water was quiet, and He brought them to their desired haven." What I found to be amazing but despaired is that God wants to be a part of your life. He wants to help you, so why do you hesitate when today is the day? Psalm 37:3–4 says, "Trust in the Lord and do good so shall you dwell in the land, and verily, you shall be fed. Delight yourself also in the Lord, and He shall give you the desires of your heart." As people, most of the time, we delight ourselves in things that fail and don't last forever, but we can move our minds off earthly things and switch them to God's eternal things.

John I 2:15–17 says, "Do not love the world or anything in the world. If anyone loves the world, love for the Father is not in them, for everything in the world—lust of the flesh, lust of the eyes, and the pride of life—comes not from the Father but from the world. Everything in this and its desires will pass away, but whoever does the will of God lives forever." The world can never satisfy our deepest longing, but if we choose to delight in God's way, He will always provide above and beyond our expectations. Always pray. You can't give up, and you can't pray sometimes only when you think about it. I am saying to get your prayer to move it. It's got to be consistent. You've got to have faith. You've got to expect to receive what you are praying.

Matthew 6:5–8 says, "And when you pray, you shall not be as the hypocrites are, for they love to pray standing in the synagogues and in the corner of the streets that they may be seen of men. Verily, I say unto you, they have their reward. But you, sincere believer, when you pray, enter into your closet, and when you have, shut your door. Pray to your Father which is in secret and shall reward you openly. But when you pray, use not vain repetition, as the heathens do, for they think that they shall be heard for their speaking. Be not you therefore like them, for your Father knows what things you have need of before you ask Him."

10

Invisible God

I know you have questions, such as "Who are you praying to? Does prayer change anything? What I am praying for?" There are so many questions with no answers. Let's start here. Did you wake up this morning? I know someone who did not wake up, even though the alarm went off, so you should be praying to God and thanking Him for allowing you to see another day. The question is "Why pray?" My answer is "Why not?"

To tell you the truth, there have been things you have done in your life, and you really did know why, perhaps because everyone else was doing it. Whatever the reason, it doesn't matter. Prayer does not fall in those areas. Prayer stands alone. It is vital, so what I am saying is you have to pray, and no, you don't see God physically, but you are made in that invisible God's image, and you can't breathe without Him. So let me be straight with you. Whether you start praying today or tomorrow, you will get the "memo." Our invisible God has an appointed time for all things, and believe me, you don't want to miss your appointment. Jesus prayed, Abraham prayed, Moses prayed, and many more in the Bible prayed. Prayer affects your life and your circumstances and the situations that you may encounter. The words or the expression "Just live" will answer all the questions you have related to "Why pray?"

Six years ago, my sister was diagnosed with cancer, but first, I think you should meet her. Shirley is a wife, a mother, and a fantastic minister who will keep you on your toes. Most likely, Ms. Cancer didn't know whom she was dealing with, so she attacked my sister's uterus. Maybe Ms. Cancer did not do her background check because she would have found that we rock and roll with the Master. Ms. Cancer screwed up and messed up. We went to the Master.

I know Ms. Cancer started wondering, "Who is that woman who sits in that pink recliner? This woman is crazy. She prays all day long. I have to found out about her, that Shirley mother, this woman who sits at her Master's feet and calls Him her 'instant Master.' Her children are also crazy. They are following in their mother's footsteps. They pray too much. I have to move."

To make a long story short, eight years today, my sister is more powerful than she has ever been because of prayer. God spoke, and every six months, she faced doctors with that the world did not give her, cancer free, so she spread the goodness of the Lord near and far, wherever she went.

There is no way you can live on this earth today and not pray, and so if you are, I wish you well. Prayer has a vital influence on our families and everything else in our lives. "Why pray?" you ask—because He died for you, and yet you think it is just another task for you to add in your busy schedule, or maybe you never had a reason to pray because everything in your life is *so* good. Every morning, as I mute my alarm clock, I make God a part of every aspect of my life. I cannot do anything without God. I need Him to hold my hands, guide me, protect me, and walk and talk with me. I can go on and on about this, but I am sure about one thing. You don't want to live without this assurance. This 100 percent–guaranteed customer service never closes. That is what God represents. "Why pray?" Because that invisible God is the Creator of everything on Earth, and He is also your provider, so when you think about it, you are not your provider. It's the invisible God, and the credit for everything you have done goes to Him.

Let me tell you a little more about my God. You think He is invisible, but He has known you since you were in your mother's womb.

God carried your parents, and now He is carrying you. God protected your parents, and now He is protecting you. *God is the one, the only one!* Come on. Let me tell you more about the invisible God. He calmed the storm. He fed five thousand. He walked on water, turned water to wine, healed the sick, and raised the dead. *Is that enough?* There is no one you know who can do anything like this but our Father in heaven.

No, God is not invisible. God is real, and He is coming back. He says so in His word, and I hope you are ready for His return. FYI, I don't think you have all the time in the world because we are like bubbles, and we are popping everywhere, young and old, and this is not your home. "When everything is ready, I will come and get you so that you will always be with me where I am" (John 14:3). God will do just what He says. That is a promise. There is no forgetting. There is no letting it slide and saying, "I'm sorry." He's just not that kind of God. He is a God of His word only, and time is passing by.

11

Just a Little Faith

Faith is a five-letter word that is so powerful, and it is something that we as God's people often lack. The meaning of faith is belief or confidence, believing and having confidence in the words that you hear. Truly, it is believing in something that you have not seen, as though it were already a reality. Most of us don't know we are living by faith daily and that it is impossible to please God without faith. My parents, bless their souls, lived by faith. They had nothing *but* God. Every day they believed and trusted in Him, and God heard their cries, and He dried their tears. I can hear my mother saying, "What a mighty God we serve."

Faith was something I always asked her about. My mother would say so many people claim they have faith until trials and tribulations come, and they run all over town trying to get help from friends and family when God is right there. Ask God for faith. Many times, I would come home, lie on Mama's red sofa in her den, fall asleep with my mouth open for two hours or more, and then wake up and tell my mother about my problems.

Lord, I can see her sitting in her pink recliner with a smile on her face, saying, "On this journey with God, you need faith, not the faith that changes from day to day—shaken faith. You need steadfast and unmovable, spiritually grounded faith, not tossed back and forth or blowing here and there and everywhere."

This lady had so much wisdom and knowledge about God. Her testimonies were like no other, and her visions and dreams would touch your soul. *"And her faith would move mountains, and there is nothing God won't do for you if you trust in Him and believe Him."* She would tell me, "Trust in Him. *I don't care how it looks or what others may say. I promise He will show up."*

Growing up, I saw that faith—unmovable faith, grounded faith, unshakable faith—when my father died. You can say what you want to, but my mother knew God, and I saw it for myself. There is something about faith in Mark 11:12–25:

> As they were passing by in the morning, they saw the fig tree withered from the root up. Being reminded, Peter said to Him, "Rabbi, look. The tree which you cursed has withered." And Jesus answered, saying to them, "Have faith in God. Truly, I say to you, whoever says to the mountain, 'Be taken up and cast into the sea,' and does not doubt in his heart but believes that what he says is going to happen, it will be granted. Therefore, I say to you, all things for which you pray and ask, believe that you have received them, and they will be granted to you."

Believe this or not, *but faith and belief lead to personal growth and success. Faith is an important part of our lives because faith comes from hearing. So what are you hearing?* Who are you keeping company with? Is that person positive or negative? I hope the answer is positive. I hope that you are hearing God's words because we will at one time or another. We must endure storms, adversity, and so much more on this earth, so whatever you have been hearing and listening to will come out of your mouth because it is stored in your heart. So when we say negative or positive things about anything, they come from our hearts.

Surely, you do know that your tongue has power. Have you ever heard this? You may think it but don't speak it because we bring life to the words we speak. You apply for a job, and they call you in for an interview. Two days before or the day of the interview, you start thinking and saying, "I want to get this job because of this or that," so if you receive a phone call and hear what you were saying, it shouldn't surprise you because you were expecting that result, for you spoke, and it came true. We say so many negative things throughout our lives, and we just don't know that our tongue can destroy our future. The devil goes around every second, every minute, and every hour of the day, stealing things from us, sometimes without us realizing it. The devil enters or injects thoughts into our minds to steal peace, joy, and even belief. "Not only does the thief come to steal, but Jesus said that he also comes to kill" (Proverbs 18:21). He says life and death are in the power of the tongue.

What is your saying about your future? What are you saying about your finances? What are you saying about your family? On my journey, I have encountered statements that were not good, such as "I am poor," "I will never be healed," "I am ugly," "I am a failure," "I will never find love," "God doesn't love me," and "I am going to lose my job." *All this is the devil.* We cannot say things like this. God created all things by His word. God spoke, and it was done, and everything He created was good. There was no mistake or misprint. We were created in His image, and we received His traits. Every day we can wake up saying positive things about our lives and expect them to happen. Our mindset can always be of God, so if you are walking and talking with God, everything in your heart is of God.

12

I Came to Save

It is erroneous to think you can believe in anything but God when you can see that nothing lasts forever and that all things will pass away. That is a promise. Still, you put your trust in man when man will leave this world also. God will give you something only He can give you: eternal life. You will never perish, so why can't you believe in God?

> Take my yoke upon you and learn from me, for I am gentle and humble in heart, and you will find rest for your souls, for my yoke is easy, and my burden light. Put everything in me first, your God, and everything will be added.

He is your Creator. He has been here since He created the world and will be here at the end. Many have heard of Him but don't know Him. You must spend time with Him to get to know Him—reading and studying your Bible, going to church, praying, learning His words, doing things God's way, not man's way. A relationship with God is the most important thing in life, and nothing will last but your relationship with Him—*nothing. Believe this because He is coming back.* Yes, this is a relationship like no other. This relationship comes with executive privileges. In this relationship, you never have to look for Him. He's always at your side. Just call His name. This relationship brings joy, peace, and happiness. Finally, it is a relationship that makes you run to tell the world how good God is. My God died on the cross for you and me. They stretched Him wide. He hung His head, and then He died. That's *love*. That's not the way the story ends though. Three days later, He rose again. That's *real love*. With all this love, who can have a seasonal, part-time, or no relationship with God? After all, He knows everything.

So what kind of relationship do you have with God? Let's see which one you fit in. "Seasonal relationship"—*Christmas, Easter, and Mother's Day* are so special to you, *so you're seen in church only on those days*. This is when you worship God. You start shopping early for your clothes because you want to look good. You haven't been to church since last year. You get a chance to talk to friends and family you haven't seen in a while, and you're very enthusiastic and happy as you put your ten or twenty dollars in the collection basket for the entire year. How crazy is it to have a seasonal relationship with God when there is adversity in your life and when you call on the Lord, you expect an answer *right now*?

Part-time in the working world means thirty hours or less in a pay period, and there are twenty-four hours in a day. So you give God some of your time, thinking basically, it's better than no time, and you go to church *sometimes* and give an offering *sometimes*, and you spend some time with Him *sometimes* because *yes*, God does know your situation and your heart. However, the question is is that the kind of relationship you want with God, your Creator, who knows everything, controls everything, predetermines everything, and does not change? He gave us free will. We have the ability to plan and make decisions, and we make the decision to be in certain situations. Just think if God decided to be just "sometimes" too.

There is this old saying: "If you know better, you do better." To you tell the truth, God doesn't make you do anything. He sits high and looks low, watching you make one mistake after another and never learn anything from them. Then He shakes His head while watching "Ms. Proud Mary" as she tries to fix things on her own, as everything falls apart around her, but she's too proud—and let's not forget "Mr. Proud Frank." He wants everyone to think he is everything when he has nothing, and what he does have, he is trying hard to keep. He's bragging about what he has, but when he shuts his doors, reality swoops in. We go through so many things when we really don't have to. God's arms are wide open. He wants a relationship with you—but not just any kind of relationship. God wants an intimate one, a continual daily walk with Him that is priceless, that builds your faith and trust in Him so that you depend on Him completely, regardless of your circumstances.

> For you are holy people, dedicated to the Lord your God. He has chosen you from all the people on the face of the whole earth to be His own chosen ones. He didn't choose you and pour out His love upon you because you were a larger nation than any other, for you were the smallest of all. It was just because He loves you and because He kept His promise to your ancestors. This is why He brought you out of slavery in Egypt with such amazing power and mighty miracles. Understand, therefore, that the Lord your God is the faithful God who, for a thousand generations, keeps His promises and constantly loves those who love Him and who obey His commands. But those who hate Him shall be punished publicly and destroyed. He will deal with them personally. Therefore, obey all these commandments I am giving you today. Because of your obedience, the Lord your God will keep His part of the contract which, in his tender love, he made with your Father. And He will love you and bless you and make you into a great nation. He will make you fertile and give fertility to your ground and to your animals so that you will have large crops of grain, grapes, and olives and great flocks of cattle, sheep, and goat when you arrive in the land He promised your father to give you. You will be blessed above all the nations of the earth. Not one of you, whether male or female, shall be barren, not even your cattle. (Deuteronomy 7:6–14)

God promises never to fail. We don't recognize that God is all and everything we need. Please put God first.

13

God's Timing, Not My Timing

Maybe you have said to yourself, "I prayed and prayed, and God never answers my prayers." You are not alone. God is different. He knows everything, and He knows what we need and when we need it. We can't understand God's timing, but He has perfect timing. He's never too early, never too late. He's just right on time. We all have heard, "*You can't rush God*," so we pray and wait, and that doesn't feel good as most of us quit because *we have no patience at all*. God specializes in patience, so while you are waiting, God is rebooting, restarting, restoring things in our hearts because He sees what is in our hearts, and yes, sometimes our hearts are far from God, and there is no fooling Him.

Patience is a fruit of the Spirit that brings about change, and change is a process. In this process, you learn how to lean and depend on God, to *trust Him and believe Him*. Trust and timing work together. Ecclesiastes 3:1 says, "To everything, there is a season, a time for every purpose under heaven." *Timing* and *season* are words that cause us to say, "*When?*" God tells us *when*. He gives us dreams, but He never says *when*. So we have to accept His timing, which is difficult most of the time because we want it *now*. Timing makes a difference in everything God does in His preparations. Yes, God does give you whatever you want, but it must be according to His *plan*, and if it's in His plan, God will prepare you to receive it.

Let me tell you a little story that only God and I know. I have been praying for God to use me since I was eighteen. It's a well-kept secret that one day I went to the store for something, and I came back with a notebook and a pack of ink pens, thinking, *I could give this to my son.* I was about thirty-seven, and I didn't like writing much, wasn't in school any longer, and had no clue. So I believe that perhaps I was going through something that day or just didn't know what to buy and picked up anything. As time passed, I found myself needing to write things down, so my son never got the notebook or the pens. What's up with this? I never really thought much about it, even when I was getting up at 3:00 a.m. to write. Call me a fool, but I did this for years. I had a notebook of lyrics, just writing what was in my heart, and I never put two and two together. This was crazy, and you may think I'm crazy because I didn't understand it myself. I'm just putting the pieces together now at the age of fifty-six. I was in the waiting room for a while, but while I was there, God was preparing me, He was restoring me. He was fixing me.

So when God spoke to me early one Sunday morning and said, "I am giving you something, so don't be afraid to tell the world what I have done for you," I jumped off the sofa, crying and running around the house, shouting because it was my time, and I will never forget that day as long as I live. This happened on a Sunday, and oh boy, later that afternoon, I spoke to my brothers, sisters, and friends. Three weeks later, God told me to write a book, and He also gave me the title.

Then came my protests. "Lord, I've never written a book before. It's going to take forever to write a book." My mind jumped from one thing to another.

Like a father, He brought back my memories. He brought back dreams I had thrown away. God's timing was awesome, and right now, I feel like the songwriter—"Lord, whatever You are doing in this season, don't do it without me, please." I just want God to use me in whatever way He wants to. You may say that was a long time to pray and wait, *but oh, I knew He was going to show up. I had no doubt at all.*

Please don't give up on God. Wait on Him. Put your trust in Him. *Know in your heart that if it is God's will, you will receive what you are praying for, and if it is not in His will, God will give you what you need in His will, and all this will happen in God's timing, not yours.* If you find yourself in the waiting room, please continue to pray and forget about time. God's got you. Daniel 10:1–21 talks about Daniel's prayer being answered but delayed, yet the archangel Michael reassured Daniel that God is *never late.* He is always on time. So take your eyes off the clock. God's time is not yours. Just keep on praying.

14

There's Something About Prayer

I am not a preacher. I don't have "Dr." in front of my name, and I am not a writer. I *am* a messenger of *the Lord*, spreading the message *that we must pray*. Jesus prayed. He would disappear for three or four hours to pray, and *He was* on this *earth*. He left special instructions always to pray, but somehow you didn't receive His "memo." At the beginning of the book, I talked about my foundation in prayer as a child, and the name my parents would call out was *"Jesus. Jesus. Jesus,"* so that stayed in my heart and is still there today.

On my journey, I found out that things can come into your life that make you put God last and every other thing first. *To be honest*, there were moments in my life when I was off and on with my prayer, and things started changing as time passed, and I was on a roller-coaster ride. So I began to have problems with things that I thought I had down pat on my job and in my finances. The first thing I said to myself was that the devil never stops, but sometimes we give the devil too much credit because sometimes it is God, and, believe this or not, God knows how to get your attention. God has a road map for everyone's life, and when you take a detour, He puts you back on course, or sometimes He takes you back to the very beginning. This, I can tell you. Yes, Lord, I started on the right highway but then began to think that things that were taking God's time had to go. I watched things happen in my life with my eyes open, and I couldn't do anything about it. We *think* we have control over the things in our lives, but we *don't*.

My mother was living at this time, and she was my ear. Every day or even twice a day I would call her, and she would say, "*Hold on*. God has a plan. You can't see it. Just keep on praying, believing, and trusting because God hears you."

As my mother spoke, her words would touch my heart because I knew she was right. *Still, sometimes, as the tears ran down my face, all her encouraging words wouldn't help, but oh, I thought if I could hear just one word from Him, it would make everything all right.* Throughout, God remained silent. I continued to fast and pray, and my relationship with Him grew stronger, but one Tuesday, at 5:00 a.m.—it's like it was yesterday—I heard a voice like no other, and still today, it lives in my heart. *You may say that I'm crazy, but He woke me up around 5:00 a.m. with a strong feeling that I needed to write* as He put the words in me. I always kept papers and a pen at my bedside. My titles of my first book and my second book, *The Movement of Prayer* and *The Waiting Room: God's Instruction Is Like No Other*, I just can't explain. So you can say I write just because it is given to me.

My relationship with God has brought changes in every area in my life. There were times in my life when I didn't know where I belonged, and I'm sure I'm not the only one who has felt that way, but I did know my purpose here on Earth. There's just *something about prayer* because all the blank spots in my life are filled now. Yes, prayer opens and closes doors. Prayer turns situations around. Prayer will make your husband, wife, and children act right. Prayer will let you pay your bills when there is no money to be found. Prayer changes CT scan results. Prayer heals. Prayer moves things around. Prayer makes your enemies behave. Prayer turns wrong into right. Prayer will see you through. I am a living witness to what prayer can do, and if you are reading this book, you are a witness to the movement of prayer as God leads me and guides me through unfamiliar territory—and it is not in nursing. So as He leads me, I ask myself and say to myself, *God girdles my hands tighter*. Yes, there is something about prayer. Prayer makes you push. Vanessa Bell Armstrong said prayer still works ("Good News"), and then she brings me down to my knee when she sings "Nobody But Jesus." Truly, saint, this is real. Lord, where would we be? What would happen if we didn't have You? We are nothing without You.

15

Does God Answer Prayers?

God is our healer, our protector, and our provider. Really, you must know He answers prayers. God is everything. God is saying yes every second, every minute, and every hour, all day and every day. That's the kind of God we serve. We are made in God's image, and He gave man dominion over His earth, so *we must pray* for sure. Prayer is the expression of man's relationship with God. On a Christian journey, we all know that God answers prayers, but we also know He does not answer *all* prayers. There are times when God says, "Yes," "Wait," and "No." The question is does your earthly father say yes to everything you ask for? If the answer is "Yes, every time," all I can say is "What a blessing!" It has never happened in my life, so we can move on.

There were times when I was unhappy with God and couldn't understand the way He thinks and His silent treatment when I knew He heard me. There are Christians who believe when they pray for something that God is going to say yes because they pay their tithes and offerings and go to church. *What does that have to do with your relationship with God? Many of you are just going through the motions, and your hearts are far from God, and God knows it.* Yes, we pray for things, and we don't believe ourselves that they're going to happen, *but we must believe it when we want to receive it.* Some pray and ask God for things that are selfish or for the wrong motives or just to inflate their egos. He is not that kind of God. We can't hide from God. Sometimes our hearts keep God from hearing *the prayers we want Him to answer. Sin is like that too.* It is hard to have a real relationship with God when your heart is not right, and yet you still want God to say yes when you hate your sister or your brother.

We were created to pray. God wants to be in your life, to walk and talk with you and guide your footsteps. God wants to say yes, but your relationship with Him has got to be right, not sometimes or part-time or none of the time. It must be right all the time, nonstop. *No matter what you are praying for, you know God is working it out for your good, and you will come through.* So when His answer to your prayer is "Yes," hallelujah! When your answer is "Wait," just say, "Fix it, Lord," and when it is "No," say, "Thank you, Lord, for watching over me" *because He knows what's best for you.*

Matthew 7:7–8 says, "Ask, and it shall be given you. Seek, and you shall find. Knock, and it shall be opened unto you. For everyone who asks will receive, and he who seeks finds, and to him who knocks, it shall be opened." Don't ever stop knocking. I promise you, the door will open. Keep your eyes on God, for He will come through. Let me take you down memory land:

> Peter was arrested and put in prison for preaching the Gospel, placing him under the guard of sixteen soldiers. Herod's intention was to deliver Peter to the Jew for execution after the Passover. But earnest prayer was going up to God from the church for his safety the whole time he was in prison. The night before he was to be executed, he was asleep, double-chained between two soldiers, with another standing guard before the prison gate, when suddenly, there was a light in the cell, and an angel of the Lord stood beside Peter. The angel slapped him on the side to awaken him and said, "Quick! Get up!" And the chain fell from his wrist. Then the angel told him, "Get dressed and put on your shoes." And he did. "Now put on your coat and follow me!" the angel

ordered. So Peter left the cell, following the angel. But the whole time, he thought it was a dream or vision and didn't believe it was really happening. They passed the first and second cell block and came to the iron gate to the street, and this opened to them of its own accord. So they passed through and walked together for a block, and then the angel left him. (Acts 12:4–11)

Let's continue down memory land. Hezekiah prays because God tells him that he is about to die.

Hezekiah now became deathly sick, and Isaiah the prophet went to visit him. "Set your affair in orders and prepare to die," Isaiah told him. "The Lord says you won't recover." Hezekiah turned his face to the wall "O Lord," he pleaded, "remember how I've always tried to obey you and to please you in everything I do. . ." Then he broken down and cried. So before Isaiah had left the courtyard, the Lord spoke to him again. "Go back to Hezekiah, the leader of my people. And tell him that the Lord God of his ancestor David has heard his prayer and seen his tears. I will heal him, and three days from now, he will be out of bed and at the temple." And God added fifteen years to his life and saved him and this city from the king of Assyria. (2 Kings 20)

So I am hoping you have your answer because God is answering prayers and opening doors every day, but you must seek God for yourself to truly know the answer for yourself. I could sit all day and tell you about my God and my testimonies, but that is my story. You need your own story. Your relationship with God will build your story and your testimonies. Yes, I can pray for you, and you can pray for me, and we can watch God change things. God loves when we pray for one another and love one another.

16

The Lord's Prayer

So when you are working with faith in God, impossible things become possible. You can speak to your mountain and say, "Move," with no doubt in your heart that it will move. The model prayer that Jesus taught his disciples in the Gospel of Matthew was given in the Sermon on the Mount. He emphasized that prayer should not be an attempt to get God's attention by repeating words. Instead, it should be a quiet, confident expression of need to our heavenly Father. Our attitude in prayer is important, and in the Sermon on the Mount, Jesus showed his disciples how to pray.

> Our Father who art in heaven, hallowed be Your name.
> Your kingdom come, Your will be done on Earth as it is
> in heaven. Give us this day our daily bread and forgive
> us our sins, for we also forgive everyone who is indebted
> to us, and do not lead us into temptation but deliver us
> from the evil one.

Our Father is the Creator of all things, Master of the universe with all power in His hand—Jehovah Jireh, my Provider, Jehovah Nissi, my Lord who reigns in victory, Jehovah Shalom, my Prince of Peace.

"Our Father who art in heaven"—heaven is God's dwelling place. He sits high and looks low. By saying, "Our Father in heaven," you're saying to God, "I recognize that I need Your help."

"Hallowed be Your name"—*hallowed* means worshipping the Father, the Holy One.

"Your kingdom come, Your will be done on Earth as it in heaven." We are asking Him what He wants done. God loves when you pray for other people, asking Him, helping and reaching out with love to others, putting yourself last and others first. "Give, and it will be given to you" (Luke 6:38). Put God's kingdom first.

"Give us our daily bread." We need God in all areas of our life: physical, spiritual, and mental. These are the daily basic needs of life. "Request only bread we cultivate. Do not be anxious, saying, 'What shall we eat?' or 'What shall we drink?' or 'What shall we put on,' for your Father knows that you need all these things. Seek first the kingdom of God, and His justice and all these things shall be given."

"Forgive us our sins, for we also forgive." The forgiveness of sins is so important to our lives. In God's eyes, we commit an enormous number of sins in our lifetimes, yet He is forgiving us continually. "For if you forgive men when they sin against you, your heavenly Father also will forgive you, but if you do not forgive men their sins, your Father will not forgive your sins" (Matthew 6:14–15). He wants to answer your prayers. As children of God, one way we can show Him our gratitude is to forgive others as He forgives us.

"Do not lead us into temptation." We are asking God to lead us and guide us the way that He wants us to go because we get in situations that compromise our relationship with God and make wrong decisions, so we need to pray for wisdom and guidance. Watch and pray so that you will not fall into temptation. The spirit is willing, but the body is weak.

"But deliver us from evil." Rescue us from Satan, cover us, and protect us from all sin and harm. God knew that His children would be tested because Jesus was tested in the wilderness. He knows we are weak, but He is strong. He knows we fall short daily, so we must pray daily and stay in God's will.

"For thine is the kingdom and the power and the glory forever and ever, amen." For this is His kingdom, and we give Him all the power and all the glory forever. He controls everything. Every word that was spoken from God's mouth is alive. The moment you accepted God in your life, your life changed, so without a doubt, we should thank God constantly for what He has done for us. A daily prayer life in a relationship with God is essential in our lives.

17

We Ought to Say Thank You

The joy to wake up and hear the birds, see the trees, breathe in the fresh air, and just hold a cup of hot coffee as the aroma takes over the space—what a moment! My daddy would sit at the kitchen table with his coffee and two pieces of toast, and Mama would be standing at the kitchen sink. Daddy would say, "Lee, we made it. This is a new day," and my mama would respond, "Thank you, Lord."

Truly nothing, was taken for granted. They knew who their protector, provider, and healer was. God created heaven and the earth. He created everything that exists on this earth. He is the provider for every creation on this earth, and He is your provider also. Please don't forget to say thank you. Sometimes we go around thinking that we are our providers, giving credit to ourselves when we have done nothing. Everything you have, God gave to you, and that includes the air we breathe. So He deserves the highest praise. He deserves the honor. He deserves the thank-you that makes you clap your hands, that makes you stomp your feet, that makes you shout, that keeps you moving—"I just can't sit down"—that makes you tell somebody about the goodness of the Lord, and when you want to do wrong, it makes you do right.

He is a "show off" God. When you're down with no dollar in your pocket, a check shows up in the mail. What a God we serve! There is a song I sang, and the words are "If you wake up in the morning, clothed in your right mind, you ought to say, 'Lord, oh, Lord, thank you.' When you are sitting at the noonday table, eating the food *God* gave you, you ought to say thank you." So how many truly wake up and say *thank you*? Just think about the question. Then try to go back to when and where.

Today we are living in a time where everything is fast and we are thinking, *Everything happening in my life is because of me. I am in control.* No. There is someone who sits higher and looks lower, in case you didn't know—your Creator, *God*. How can it be that we take so much for granted—waking up in your right mind, the activity of your limbs, eating, breathing, just living, the clothes on your back, parents, siblings, the roof over your head, transportation, and employment? There is always someone wishing and praying for something you are taking for granted, telling God *thank you* throughout the day It shouldn't be so hard.

I often say to myself, *I am glad God is not like man. We would be in trouble.* While I was standing in line at the cash register, a teenager asked her mother for money to buy something in the store. Once she got the money, she walked off. Her mother continued to wait while staring at her daughter, and she never said a word. I wonder if that's the way God looks at us. We probably do this sevens day a week, twenty-four hours a day. Nothing comes out of us but "what I got." A meaning of thanks is your polite expression when acknowledging a gift or accepting or refusing an offer. We never refuse anything from God.

On that note, we need to tell God thank you daily. His gifts come in many ways—nice cars, clothes. We are just blessed. God is only asking for a minute of your time. With all the blessings and shortcomings, we ought to thank God. We drive, fly, walk alone at home, at work, at school. Who is protecting you or covering you from sickness and disease, harm and danger, seen or unseen? Yes, we know things happen, good and bad, and it appears to be more negative than positive. The devil is loose, so put on your armor of God, pray daily and throughout the day, read His words, keep His words in your heart, and pray for protection, seen and unseen, over your families. Give God total control of every area of your life because He is your protection and He covers us all night. We want to say thank you.

Please don't live day in and day out thinking or assuming that things with always be the same as every other day is new. Always be grateful, and never take love for granted. Appreciate what you have before time makes you appreciate what you had. God is waiting. Tell Him thank you. This not a God you found in the cracker box. This is a living God. Tell somebody what He has done for you. Tell them He has been a mother and father for you. Tell them that He may not come when you want him to, but He is right on time. Tell them He makes a way out of no way. He told me to tell you that He is God and God all by Himself and to put your trust in Him. Believe in Him and not in any other god, for He is your provider. So stop saying you did this and that and say "I." Your God did this and that. "I am the vine, and you are the branches. Everything comes through me, your God, your protector, provider, and healer."

Psalm 34:8–9 says, "O taste and see that the Lord is good. Blessed is the man who trusts in Him. O fear the Lord, ye his saint, for there is no want to them who fear him."

18

Waiting and Praying

My mother would always say God is not a God who can be rushed, but He is right on time. She would also say we think when obstacles show up in our lives, we want them to vanish into thin air now. Well, guess what? You've got to wait on God. You can't fix it, and God doesn't need your help. I have lost many hours of sleep trying to fix things in my life. My encouraging words to you are even if God takes too long, go find a place to pray until God comes. Get on your knees and be patient, with your eyes on God, not on your situation.

Our eyes sometimes are all right. Most of the time, they add or take away from us. Let's be real. Our eyes take from us a good 70 percent of the time because it is so easy to think negatively than positively. There are many who have stopped praying after a while because they did not see anything moving. Tell me, what is your meaning of "a while"? When you are praying for something, move timing to the side and replace it with "praying with expectation." Expectation comes with regulations. First, don't care what the devil says. Two, don't care how it may look or how it may seem. You are expecting to receive what you're praying for. Yes, I see it. I am walking in faith. I am going to wait on the Lord. I am not worried about what people say. No one knows what I have been through. God kept me and still keeps me today.

We must learn how to encourage ourselves. Go back and remind yourself what God has done for you and how God shows up in your life when everyone dragged your name up and down the street, including your family's (and they had no clue). Go back to the times you had no money and no food in your refrigerator and how God showed up in the mailbox with a check or how God showed up in a hidden section in your purse and how joy filled your heart. Go back to the time your electricity was going to be cut off, how God showed up just in time. God is never late. Watch God move. Stop feeling sorry for yourself. You are not alone. You will never be alone. It just appears to be that way. So chill out. God is the same yesterday and today.

Please, let's not forget this, saint. I know every situation is different, but God is still the same. I know you feel like you've been in the waiting room for a long time. The "waiting room" is a special room, and there are many in this room, including me. We are waiting for healing, doors to be open, jobs, financial blessings, marriage, and so much more, but it is temporary. I know God's got a plan. Being in the waiting room assists with some of the things we have a little problem with, like patience. Sad to say that is a big one. "We don't have time to be waiting." Let's not mess with patience. What about love? Well, we've got problems with that one too. How could it be? God is love. I believe in the waiting room, God is fixing our hearts and minds to receive because God knows what we need.

So when God shows up, you will be ready because you want receive a text message or a phone call. God just shows up. It does matter what day or the time of the day. God brings it openly. "Let everybody see it—nothing small about my God." Don't ever stop praying. Don't ever stop believing.

19

Did God Get Your Attention?

Through all the hustle and bustle, we find less and less time to spend with God. "We want to have a good time. I just want to have a good time." Unfortunately, life is not centered on always having a good time. There are bad times too, and there are times where there is no good or bad. It's just okay. For some, it does not matter what kind of time they're going through. It never seems to cause them to pray because their heart appears to be made of stone, so they think.

Years ago, I met a young lady, and her family loved to party from Friday through Sunday, and this was every weekend. I would think, *Everything must be good in their lives, no worries or cares, just them living it up.* One Friday evening I noticed there was no music playing. The house was dark, with nothing moving. Perhaps they had gone out of town. Later that evening, I heard about the young lady I had met. Her boyfriend had shot her twice in the head. It was very sad, and my heart went out to the parents because no parent wants to bury their child.

I know sometimes things happen, but I also know so many of us are sleeping on this journey. God knows how to wake you up, and most of the time, we know when we are sleeping. When something happens in your life, you wonder why, but things happen to us all. When you have been sleeping, the first thing you think about is say to yourself, *I need to start praying.* What have you been doing? This is what we are created to do. Yes, but God is an attention seeker, and you will pay attention. There are many who think they are home free because God has not gotten their attention yet. If God has not gotten your attention yet, God is giving you a choice to seek Him first on your own. That's the kind of God we service. I laugh inside when people my age tell me they have not decided on whether God is real or not when we have one foot on the earth and the other in the grave. Most of us believe when bad things happen, it's all the devil because it seems only fair that the devil would do this. The devil has tricked you this time. *God* did this, God has been waiting and waiting for you, so now God is doing this His way. I know you don't want to hear this, but God chastises His children, and there are times when we are disobedient and hardheaded. I can honestly say you don't want play with God, period.

I am reminded of God calling Moses to return to Egypt to set His people free, and there were many Israelites in Egypt, and Pharaoh made them all slaves. God wanted to save His people, so He told Moses to go before Pharaoh and tell him to "Let my people go." Moses listened to God and agreed to go to Pharaoh. Because Pharaoh would not listen to God through Moses, God sent the plagues. A plague is a very bad thing, and God sent *ten*. For the first plague, the Nile River turned into blood. That was very important to the Egyptian people. This was their only water resource. Oh, well. The river was filled with blood that had a bad smell, and everything died in that river. People, wake up. God is not playing with you. For the second plague, frogs were everywhere, and no one could kill them because they had special powers. The third plague was gnats, the fourth plague flies, the fifth plague livestock killed, the sixth plague boils, the seventh plague a storm, the eighth plague locusts, the ninth plague darkness. Can you imagine what the tenth plague was?

All I know is that God is God, all by Himself, and God's words have existed from the beginning of time. His words have stayed the same. They have never changed. So how do we believe that what we do doesn't carry consequences? So how do we believe that God will look over this or that or the way you live? If it is not pleasing to God, put it in the right place so you can please your Father. This starts today because tomorrow might be too late. There are so many people waiting. Why can't you go to God now? Why has God got to get your attention to make you get to know Him? Why don't you want to know God? What are you doing? You can't be sleeping when everything is falling around you. Get up. God is coming. Put things in order.

In the Bible, everywhere Jesus went, people were waiting, crowds of people. Miracles were happening everywhere. There was healing and blessing everywhere, and those same miracles are happening today. You probably would disagree with me, but it is true. Someone is being healed every day. Someone is ringing the bell every day, completing their chemotherapy and being cancer free. Someone who was lost is now found. Someone who had negative results in their CT and MRI scans now has positive results. All kinds of miracles are happening daily. So why has God got to get your attention to worship and praise Him with your whole heart?

Yes, I know there are nonbelievers everywhere, and there are many who worship all kinds of idols and gods. I would not go there if I were you. What you need to do is to run to the church and ask, "What must I do to be saved?" while you have a chance. Stop listening to Sue and Bobby because God gets our attention individually, and no one will be able to bring peace and joy back in your life but God. I know everyone's situation is different and we all were brought up differently, but we all sit on our tubs alone. You came into this world alone.

Many say, "My parents did not take me to church." Okay, you're grown up. What now? I can imagine the things people will be saying when they stand before God, when God asks, "Why did you not worship me, and why didn't you live by my words?" All kinds of things will be said. "I had to work. I had to take my kids to practices. I had so much to do. My son used the car to go to work. I was going through a lot with my husband." All these excuses have no value when it comes to God. God's got to get your attention to worship Him when God is the only one providing what you need, and you can't serve God. When was the last time you said thank you to God? I hope you are smiling because if man was God, you would be messed up because whatever has gotten you not worshipping or situations that were taking your time, that would be your god, and it would have to supply your needs. Yes, I know you would get things corrected. It's just funny how we prefer God getting our attention, not knowing how God is going to get our attention. I wish you luck on that.

20

The Magical Name of Jesus

There is something about the name Jesus. The name Jesus would ring in the morning, noon, and day when my parents say "Jesus" in their prayers. It was so forceful and powerful. It could have broken anything apart. In no way could mountains move through prayer by just saying Jesus's name and expecting anything to happen. You've gotten used to the authority behind that name. To get results, you've got to have a relationship with Him.

Praying in the name of Jesus gives our prayer power, but sometimes the magical name of Jesus does give you what you prayed for. Because it must be in His will, the magical name of Jesus is powerful, but there is another component that must be there for the power to work: faith, as small as a mustard seed. That should be very easy to achieve, don't you think? But it is not because that little faith can move mountains, and sometimes our faith starts to wave everywhere. When you are faced with life's mishap, you start questioning God.

One year ago, I stood in an unfamiliar place where my heart was attacked with fear, knowing God was there the whole time and hearing, "There was something found on your mammogram, and we need you to come in tomorrow. We will be doing another mammogram, okay?"

As I was getting in my car, I shouted, "Jesus!" like I had never shouted before. Oh, the power of my shout took me to my knees as I called my Father in heaven's name. My faith stood up, bold and strong, as I refreshed my memory of God's promise to me and prayed. I prayed that I was not going to let God go until He blessed me. It was morning, a new day, and God was still the same as yesterday. I arrived thirty minutes early, eager to get this done.

My name was called, so while the mammogram was being done, the tech said to me, "Whatever was on there yesterday is gone. Let me look at yesterday's results again."

Two other techs showed up. There was nothing. Later, the doctor talked to me to confirm that I was good to go until next year. There is no one who can tell me what God can't do. I know God personally for myself, so when you see me and I am smiling, it's all God.

Oh, how I love Jesus because He first loved me! My parents would sing that song so much, bless their souls. It helped them get through whatever they were going through. Do you have a song? Everyone should have a song to help you get through. My song is "I Need Thee Every Hour." The magical name Jesus is everlasting. Mirror, mirror on the wall, what is the greatest name of all? Jesus—a name given to Him by God, His heavenly Father, which *means "savior,"* God's Son, who came to the earth as a human to save God's people from sin. Oh, there is something about his name!

John 6:35 says, "Jesus said, 'I am the bread of life.'" John 7:37 says, "If anyone is thirsty, let him come to me and drink." John 14:6 says, "Jesus said, 'I am the way, yes, and the truth and the life. No one can get to my Father except by means of me.'" John 14:12–13 says, "In solemn truth, I tell you, anyone believing in me shall do the same miracle I have done and even greater ones because I am going to be with the Father. You can ask Him for anything using my name, and I will do it, for this will bring praise to the Father because of what I, the Son, will do for you. Yes, ask anything using my name, and I will do it."

What a name that brings about power during the storm when faith and belief are there too! To believe and have faith is what you need to move mountains, but to believe is also a challenge for many. I know you don't want to believe this. When trying times show up, that is when we find out about our level of belief. God gives instructions to many of us every day. Most of us overlook what is being said, and the others don't believe what has been said. "Something came to me, but I can't do that." You can't do that because you don't believe that God can make this happen for you. There are many today who are not where God wants them to be because of nonbelief, and you quit to say, "I've always wanted to do this or that." To walk with faith and belief is a blessing, and it comes from hearing the words of God. The magical name of Jesus casts the devil out of many, moves mountains, causes walls to fall, heals the sick, gives sight to the blind, and so much more. You've got to get to know Him, saints.

> If you love me, obey me, and I will ask the Father, and He will give you another Comforter, and He will never leave you. He is the Holy Spirit, the Spirit who leads into all truth. The world at large cannot receive Him, for it isn't looking for Him and doesn't recognize Him. But you do, for He lives with you now and someday shall be in you. No, I will not abandon you or leave you as an orphan in the storm. I will come to you. In just a little while, I will be gone from the world, but I will still be present with you. For I will live again, and you will too. When I come back to life again, you will know that I am in my Father and you in me and I in you. The one who obeys me is the one who loves me, and because he loves me, the Father will love him, and I will too, and I will reveal myself to him. (John 14:15–21)

Jesus is a name that was given from God, His heavenly Father, a name that has the meaning of "savior." He came with a purpose to save. Let's see. We all have names, and our names have meanings. I think we all have a purpose. So tell me—what is your purpose? Do you have a clue? I am just asking because you were chosen and you are loved by God.

21

Move, Get Out of My Way

How can you come to church and sit on God after everything God has done for you? Sometimes I think people think God must do the things that He does for us when their mouths are closed, their arms are glued to their bodies, and their feet are stuck to the floor, just dead, but they are quick to say something about the one who is praising God because they know who their provider is. So why did you come? You are uncomfortable. Are you a spectator? Oh, I get it. "It's the right thing to do." Stay home if you're going to rain on someone's parade. Because of what God has done for me, I will run right over you, jumping, shouting, and clapping my hands—and yes, it takes all that. I don't have any shame when it comes to serving God.

I service a living God. Everything I have, God gave to me. Get out of my way. Move. I can't help it if God has not done anything for you. Move. FYI, when you enter the house of the Lord, you should be in rare form—excited, happy to be worshipping with your sisters and brothers. The choir should not have to put you in the move for praising God. All that God has done for me this week, I came with.

Make a joyful noise unto the Lord, all ye lands. Serve the Lord with gladness. Come before His presence with singing. Know ye that the Lord is God. It is He who has made us and not we ourselves. We are His people and the sheep of His pasture. Enter into His gates with thanksgiving and into His courts with praise. Be thankful unto Him and bless His name. For the Lord is good, His mercy is everlasting, and His truth endures to all generations. (Psalms 100:1–5)

So for the "dead" one who comes to church Sunday after Sunday, you need to check which god you are servicing because the god you are servicing has got to be dead. My God who wakes me up in the morning is all about us making a joyful noise. My God doesn't care for quietness. The Bible commands us to praise the Lord with music, singing, shouting, and dancing. God is worth praising. I know we are all going through something. The church is the hospital, and God is the doctor. We are supposed to leave our situations at the altar and praise and worship God and know that "He's got this." You must know this from your heart. Getting mad and depressed is not God. God is joy. Praise Him despite it all. Stop coming to church like mummies. Unwrap yourselves, open your mouths, and say, "Yes, Lord! Amen!" Move those arms, clap your hands, and stomp your feet. This is the way you do it.

> Praise the Lord! Praise the Lord, O my soul! While I live will I praise the Lord. I will sing praises unto my God while I have any being. Put not your trust in princes nor in the son of man, in whom there is no help. His breath goes forth. He returns to his earth. In that very day, his thoughts perish. Happy is he who has the God of Jacob for his help, whose hope is in the Lord his God which made heaven and earth, the sea and all that therein is, which keeps truth forever, which executes judgment for the oppressed, which gives food to the hungry. The Lord loves the prisoner. The Lord opens the eyes of the blind. The Lord raises them who are bowed down. The Lord loves the righteous. The Lord preserves the strangers. He relieves the fatherless and widowed, but the way of the wicked, He turns upside down. The Lord shall reign forever, even your God, O Zion, unto all generations. Praise ye the Lord. (Psalms 146:1–10)

So move, girl. Take your eyes off me and put them on God. Move. Get out of my way. Every time I turn around, He keeps blessing me, and I can't explain it. I've got to praise God. Move, girl. I am making the devil mad. Move praises. Promote productivity. Come on, move. Get off the sofa in front of the television. Move. Get out of the recliner. Move if God has done anything for you move. Stop sitting on God.

Tell someone what God has done for you, and when they ask why you are moving like that, tell them, "Every time I turn around, God keeps blessing me. That is what God does. I met a man called Jesus many years ago from Galilee. He told me that He would set me free, that He could make the impossible possible. I met a man—yes, Jesus, who never let me down, who dried my weeping eyes and never stopped loving me no matter what! I am going to praise Him for the rest of my life, and guess what? I don't care if you don't praise God because you are not taking from my praise, so all who move and shake for God, let's do this."

22

Happy People

God's people are happy people. We can sing and dance all week long. "This little light of mine, I'm gonna let it shine! This little light of mine, I'm gonna let it shine! This little light of mine, I'm gonna let it shine, let it shine, shine, shine, let it shine! Everywhere I go, I'm gonna let it shine! Everywhere I go, I'm gonna let it shine! Everywhere I go, I'm gonna let it shine, let it shine, shine, shine, let it shine!" All over the world, happy people are entering God's gates with thanksgiving. Everyone is happy, hugging and kissing, glad to be in God's house one more time. Yes, when all of God's children get together, what a time we have! Some of our hearts are aching and full of pain, disappointment, and so much more, but there's just something about worship. When all God children come together. we get a little stronger to fight a little longer.

When I woke up this morning, the sun was shining so bright, with not a cloud nowhere. It brought a smile on my face, and I told the Lord, "Thanks for this day." It was not about the sun shining. It was about God waking me up to see the sun shine. It is all about God's promise and His blessings that shower light upon us, that shine wherever we go and bring happiness during tribulations. When you are crying, you should be smiling because God is with you. For many, the devil has stolen their shine. Even when they know God fed the hungry, healed the sick, put clothes on their backs, and sheltered and protected them from all harm, there is no shine, no happiness there at home, on the sofa, as they are working, washing their cars, mowing the grass. They are doing everything but going to church. Their happiness comes from what they are doing at that time, which will vanish soon. Yes, many will say, "I worship God in my heart." No. God believes in unity and togetherness. Where there are two or more, God is in their midst.

God's happiness is everlasting, with no expiration date, and not given from the world. His happiness is a gift. Those who serve the flesh as their god are just miserable because their god is vile, weak, deceitful, and transitory. So in case you try seeking happiness, that does work. The Bible says, "Seek first God's kingdom and His righteousness, and all these things will be given to you as well," and it does include joy, happiness, peace, and love. You are probably thinking, *It's just not that deep, and it's hard to find. Happiness is overrated. No one is happy today.* Well, I am feeling different about that. Just knowing God loves you should bring about happiness because every one of your needs, God will provide, and it does not cost anything. Happiness is free, and joy is free. You don't have to look anywhere. God's got it. You don't have to look toward alcohol or drugs. God's got it. He is in the business of restoration.

Being on this earth, I have noticed happiness, for most, depends on what is happening, and if there is no happening, there is no happiness. For some, we base our happiness on people and material things, and when all fails, there goes happiness. Happiness is visible. It is a feeling that can't be contained, so in case you didn't know, you can only pretend you are happy for a while. It doesn't work. God's happiness is internal, reflexive, and external. This causes others to wonder why you are always happy and what is keeping you happy. I truly believe if you take the time and think and compare where you once were to now and how God brought you, maybe you would not wonder why they are happy because now you are happy too, and if that does work, think about what God has done for you, how God made a way out of no way. Today, you are probably saying to yourself, *How can we focus on being happy when there is so much going on?* No, it is not about focusing on happiness. It is about the goodness of God and your relationship with

God. That will manifest happiness, knowing that God is with you to carry your burdens. The Bible tells us there is a season for all things. So we already know we are going to have cloudy days, rainy days, foggy days, and storms too, but the God we service causes the sun to shine in the midst of it all. Weeping may endure for a night, but joy comes in the morning. Yes, I am happy. Sing this song with me: "Joy, joy, God's great joy! Joy, joy, down in my soul! Sweet, beautiful, soul-saving joy! Oh, joy, joy in my soul!" Let's sing it again: "Joy, joy, God's great joy! Joy, joy, down in my soul! Oh, sweet, beautiful, soul-saving joy! Oh, joy, joy in my soul!"

Psalm 149 says, "Praise ye the Lord. Sing unto the Lord a new song and His praise in the congregation of the saints. Let Israel rejoice in Him who made him. Let the children of Zion be joyful in their King. Let them praise His name in the dance. Let them sing praise unto Him with the timbrel and harp. For the Lord takes pleasure in His people. He will beautify the meek with salvation. Let the saints be joyful in glory. Let them sing aloud upon their beds. Let the high praises of God be in their mouths and two-edged swords in their hands. To execute vengeance upon the heathen and punishment upon the people. To bind their kings with chains and their nobles with fetters of iron. To execute upon them the judgment written. This honor have all His saints. Praise ye the Lord."

23

Fix My Heart

There are so many things that keep God from answering our prayers. My mother was a firm believer that your heart must be right, and sometimes things can hinder our prayers. We get up every morning, put on our nice clothes and matching shoes, and tie our hair. External appearances can't touch that, but the internal is just torn up. Our hearts hold things that God is not a part of.

Sin: We sin daily. We sin in word, deed, and thought daily, and we all continue to struggle, so asking for forgiveness could be daily. "Sin separates us from God, and your iniquities have separated you from God. Your sin has hidden His face from you, so He will not hear" (Isaiah 59:2).

Fear: What we would do without fear? The unknown scares us. Fear keeps us in the darkness. It keeps us oppressed and depressed. It is not what we need in our lives. It steals from us. Fear paralyzes us and prevents growth moving forward. As God's people, sometimes we do serious things that God is not pleased with. Yes, we fall short, and fear is driven in, or the devil tells you things like "God would never forgive you." Family members and friends discourage instead of encourage you, so now you're paralyzed, and you can't move forward. As a Christian, I am here to say God will never leave you. He is right by your side. God is a forgiving God. So when you go before God, it does not matter what happened in your past. God is love. The devil is fear.

Doubt: Sometimes doubt comes easily in some Christians' daily walks. Why pray for something when, after you've finished praying, you don't believe it anyway? Why?" Doubt is the lack of confidence, and it will hold you back. Yet again, doubt comes from our minds and hearts. Doubt can appear from negative upbringing, past situation that were negative, or just finding it hard to say positive things in your life. Mark 11 says, "Jesus was hungry and approached a fig tree for some food. Finding no fig on the tree, he cursed it. Now in the morning, as he passed by him, he saw that the fig tree had dried up from the root, and Peter remembered saying to him, 'Rabbi, look. The fig tree which you cursed has withered away.' So Jesus answered and said to them, 'Have faith in God. For assuredly, I say to you, whoever says to the mountain, "Be removed and cast into the sea" and does not doubt in his heart but believes that those things he says will be done, he will have whatever he says. Therefore, I say to you, whatever thing you ask, when you pray, believe that you will receive them, and you will have them.'"

Guilt: We as people do things, and once they are done, we can't hit rewind. We must accept what was done, ask for forgiveness and really mean it, and move on—but no, that is not happening. Guilt has got you and is blocking you. God does remember your sins once they have been forgiven. He does need to remind you of your sins. God is not like man, and He doesn't think like man. God is like no other. You can search high and low, and you will find no one like God.

Bitterness: We are not perfect, and sometimes someone can say or do something, intentional or unintentional, that can really hurt us and plant a seed, and we would have no clue. So now it is hidden, which makes it dangerous. The soil of bitterness is in the heart, which harbors hostility and does deal with hurt. When someone becomes bitter, the bitterness takes root in their heart and grows deeper. Your intention is negative toward that individual. So in case you didn't know, it doesn't matter how long you pray. God won't hear you. There are many Christians today who are dealing with old hurt. We must give this to God. Let Him restore your heart. Forgive that individual and pray with a pure heart.

Unforgiveness: Come on. You want God to forgive you, but you can't forgive your sister or brother for something that happened six months or ten years ago. That sounds like a joke, but sadly, there are Christians who have left this earth and never forgiven someone. You have to forgive because it will block your relationship with God and others. Mark 11:24–25 says, "Therefore, I say unto you, what things so ever you desire, when you pray, believe that you receive them, and you shall have them. But when you are praying, first forgive anyone you are holding a grudge against so that your Father in heaven will forgive your sins too." Forgiveness is something you've got to do.

Idols: They come in many forms and shapes, large or small. An idol is an image or representation of God used as an object of worship. An idol is any person, object, or activity you give a higher priority to in your life than a relationship with God. An idol can be your home, your job, a vehicle, a relation, or even your family. An idol can be a pet, a computer, or what you look at on the computer. An idol can be alcohol, drugs, sex, or any sin. God is a jealous God, and He wants our time and attention. Exodus 20:1–6 says, "And God spoke all these words, saying, 'I am the Lord your God, which have brought you out of the land of Egypt. Out of the house of bondage, you shall have no other God before me. You shall not make unto yourself any graven image or any likeness of anything that is in heaven above or that is in the earth beneath or that is in the water under the earth. You shall not bow down yourself to them nor serve them, for I am the Lord your God, a jealous God." We must examine our lives to see what is important to us and how much time we are spending with this because God deserves everything. Today God is put on a shelf that we forgot to dust, and yes, we are His people *but* lost people. We think we have all the time in the world but really don't.

Wait! I can't forget God's people who can't open their hearts to give. I wonder what that is called—maybe "stingy." Read this: they give two or three dollars to someone they know in need and think they have done the deed of a lifetime. We also have Christians who give with a grudging heart and Christians who offer but hope you would say no. Giving comes from the heart, with nothing in return. Stinginess prevents our prayers from being heard. Proverb 21:13 says, "If a man shuts his ear to the cry of the poor, he too will cry out and not be answered."

24

God's Love Runs Deep

To all my children—young and old, male and female, poor and rich, believers and nonbelievers—I want you to know that I love you unconditionally. I love you from the moment of conception, for you were chosen. I knew you before your parents did. I have never once left your side and am still at your side this day and forever more. Still, some choose to leave me for whatever reason and seek things that are non-lasting and displeasing to me yet are content. Yes, you leave, later return, and leave again.

My child, my love remains the same. My arms open wide, and my angels watch you all day and all night. I love you. My promises are my vow to you. That will never be broken or voided. Your God came to save you, to put light in a dark place, to guide the lost who want to be found—their rock in weary land. Your God, your Father, loves you so much and came so that you might have life and have it more abundantly. Yes, there is a thief in their midst who is taking from my beloved children whom I love so much, disobedient to my words, opening the doors to enter and steal. My children, you must be obedient to your God's words. I have left the blue book, the Bible, here with you, my child. Just start with the Ten Commandments. Learn them and place every commandment deep down in your heart and live by it. To obey your God is to be blessed. To disobey is to be cursed.

Please, for me, your God, just listen to my words. You must do what I say. You would do this if you love me, your God, but first, you've got to know if you love me. Do you love me, your God? Why, my children? Why am I feeling doubt? Why am I not included in your lives, and why you do continually seek my love? I am not dead, but you treat me like I am dead, and yet I am with you everywhere you go. My children, are you studying my words? Are you worshipping and praising me, your God? Praying is a must. Also, my child, who are you servicing? Is it your God, or is it something else? Do you not see I love you? What are you listening to? Do you not know I am the way, the truth, and the life? No one comes to the Father except through me. Your God sent His only begotten Son into this world so that we might live through Him. I love you. There is no other love like my love.

Roman 5:8 says, "God demonstrates His love toward us in that while we were yet sinners, Christ died for us." The Bible says, "They stripped Him and put Him in a scarlet robe, and then they put a plaited crown of thorns upon His head and a reed in His right hand, and they bowed the knee before Him and mocked Him, saying, 'Hail, king of the Jews!' And then they spit upon Him and took the reed and smote Him on the head. After that, they took His robe off Him and put His own raiment on Him and led Him away to be crucified. The guards watched Him all night long, and there were two thieves crucified with Him, on the right and the left hand, and many who passed observed Him moving His head, saying, 'You who will destroy the temple and build it back in three days, save yourself. If you are the Son of God, come down from the cross.' The chief priest was also mocking Him along with the others, and the elder said, 'He saved others, but He could not save Himself.' Darkness took over the land around noon until the ninth hours, when Jesus cried out with a loud voice, 'My God, My God, why have You forsaken me?'" Our God died on that cross for our sins. Our God was wrapped in clean linen and laid in His own tomb. The tomb was sealed and guarded, but that could not retain our God. On the third day, God rose, with all power in His hand.

What human being would not worship or praise our God? What human being would not have faith and trust in our God? There is nothing I can say, nothing compared to our God. So we know, and that is why the Bible that is sitting on your dresser, that is surrounded with dust, should now be dusted off and opened to read. Yes, you, the one who lies on the sofa every Sunday because there is nothing to do, will now start going to church on Sunday. Here we go. To the ones who are mad with God because your marriage didn't work, and you tried so hard to make your marriage work, and you prayed, and your prayer was not answered, God knows. He knows. Smile. Be happy. God knows what He is doing. God's got a plan. I promise. Get out of bed, dress up, and go to church.

Okay, to my friends who have been laid off from their jobs, count all your joys. You are walking into a better job, so why are you not at church? To my beloved ones who don't understand why God let this or that happen—"Why, God, did you do this?"—just get up, honey. Dress up for church because God is a God whom you or anyone else will never understand, because God is the only one who sees what is down the road. Just keep praying and going to church. For the ones who have been healed from any kind of sickness, who are home and praising the doctor, let me whisper in your ear, "It was God. You could start praising God right this minute. I will see you in church." The love God has for us—seriously, everyone should be running to church with no doubt about anything when it is related to God. Did God die for nothing? Can you please ask that question to yourselves? Because of the love that God has and has shown to us, every church should be overflowing, and bible studies should be flooded. Yes, I say our God is going to prepare a place for us, and God is coming back. Please be ready.

25

Forgiving God

Thanks, God, for loving us. The Bible says, "If we confess our sins, He is faithful and just to forgive us our sins and to cleanse us from all unrighteousness" (1 John 1:9). There are one hundred Bible verses about God's forgiveness, but man is hard to forgive and often forgets. Oh, the Bible never said to forget. We have to remember. Perhaps that is why we can forgive. There are so many who have left this world and never forgiven their sister or brother for something that was done when they were kids or something that hurt their feelings, and the person never knew they had said something to anger them. Yes, but you want God to forgive you. I am spreading the word. God is a forgiving God, yet you can't forgive your wife or husband who divorced you, and it's been twenty years. Why can't we move on to the next chapter of our lives? Why have we got to hold on to the past? Stop looking back. I had a habit too of looking back. Someone asked me, "Why can't you forgive that person and move on?" Yes, sometimes we can get blind.

Matthew 6:14–15 says, "For if you forgive others their trespasses, your heavenly Father will also forgive you, but if you do not forgive others their trespasses, neither will your Father forgive your trespasses." I found out forgiving is a mover. It causes growth and happiness. Not forgiving causes too much pain. Let's not forget anger and resentment. Seriously, it's not good at all, health wise. No. Have you ever thought about the things you've done repeatedly? You constantly ask God for "forgiveness," knowing it was wrong from the beginning, but you never think God is going to get tired. Some never learn the first time. They must do severe time, and they never think there could be some consequence in the future or down the road. I am telling you, if God would have given us a set number of times for Him to forgive us, we would be a mess because most of our forgiveness would be from our thinking or thoughts.

All I know is that I am glad Peter asked the Lord, "How often shall my brother sin against me and I forgive him? Till seven times?" Jesus said unto him, "I say unto you, not until seven times but until seventy times seven." Then God went into a parable illustrating the principle of forgiveness. God told them there was a certain king who would take account of his servant, and when he had begun to check the books, one was brought unto him who owed him ten thousand talents, but for as much as he couldn't pay, his lord commanded him and his wife and children and all that he had to be sold and the payment to be made. The servant fell to the floor and worshipped him, saying, "Lord, have patience with me, and I will pay you all." Then the lord of that servant was moved with compassion, set him loose, and forgave the debt. God said that same servant went out after being forgiven, found one of his fellow servants who owed him hundred pence (which is three hundred), laid his hand on him, and took him by the throat, saying, "Pay me what you owe me." The fellow servant fell down at his feet and besought him, saying, "Have patience will me, and I will pay you all." He would not forgive him for three hundred. He went and cast him in prison until he could pay the debt. (Well, I must say today they kill for three hundred.) So when his fellow servant saw what was done, they were sorry, and it was repeated to the lord, what was done. Then his lord called him, the one who had forgiven the ten thousand talents, and reminded him that he had forgiven him for all that debt because he desired it of him. "So why could you not have compassion on your fellow servant?" His lord was very angry and delivered him to be tormented until he paid all that was due to him.

In case you didn't know, when you truly forgive someone, it must come from the heart and thrown into the sea of forgetfulness. There are many of us "Christians," and yes, we say we have forgiven that person, but every time you get in any kind of confrontation or similar situation, it brings about the past, and this was done to you, or something was said to you. Somehow it comes back from the sea because it never got to the sea of forgetfulness. It's still on land, riding with you. This is my advice to myself, and maybe you can use this too. I am not going to let anyone or anything keep me from seeing my Father's face. This place is not our home. We have just "stopped by," and only what we do for our heavenly Father will last.

Stop tripping on Maryjane. Forgive her for going to the movie with Tom, knowing you were liking Tom. Tom, be with somebody else, please. Joe, forgive Marvin for borrowing ten dollars twenty years ago and not paying you back for gas. Yes, these things appear small but carry a lot weight when compared to doing the will of God. Micah 7:18 says, "Who is a God like you, pardoning iniquity and passing over transgression for the remnant of His inheritance? He does not retain his anger forever because He delights in steadfast love." Matthew 7:21–23 says, "Not everyone who says to me, 'Lord, Lord, will I enter the kingdom of heaven?' but the one who does the will of my Father who is in heaven. On the day, many will say to me, 'Lord, Lord, did we not prophesy in your name, cast out demons in your name, and do mighty works in your name?' Then depart from me, you worker of lawlessness. Just know God is a forgiving God."

26

Let's Praise Him

(Lift Your Hands)

Lord, You have been good, and Your mercy endureth forever
People from every nation and tongue, from generation to generation
We worship You—hallelujah, hallelujah! We worship You for who You are
For You are, for You are good
Lord, You are good, and Your mercy endureth forever
Lord, You are good, and Your mercy endureth forever
People from every nation and tongue, from generation to generation
We worship You—hallelujah, hallelujah! We worship You for who You are
For You are, for You are good
Yes, You are so good, so good
You are good all the time, all the time, You are good
Lord, You are good, and Your mercy endureth forever
People from every nation and tongue, from generation to generation

Come on, praise Him!

Come on, lift your hands, and say

My hallelujah belongs to You
My hallelujah belongs to You

My hallelujah belongs to You

You deserve it
You deserve it
You deserve it
You deserve it

My hallelujah belongs to You
My hallelujah belongs to You
My hallelujah belongs to You
My hallelujah belongs to You

You deserve it
You deserve it
You deserve it
You deserve it

Hallelujah!
Hallelujah!
Hallelujah!
Hallelujah!
All the glory
All the honor
All the praise

You deserve it
You deserve it
You deserve it
You deserve

27

Sold Out for Jesus

This started out a long time ago. There is no doubt in my mind. I decided to make Jesus my choice. At the age of sixteen, my parents stood in front of God and made a vow that stood for the test of time, by living by God's words—only "sold out for Jesus"—and their steps were ordered by the Lord. Their eyes never moved off Jesus. Let me say this. Jesus was all my parents had. They did not have a 401(k). No, they didn't have a checking or saving account. Everything they had was invested in Jesus completely, but if you think about it, everything we have belongs to our Father—everything. I have found that time is a major element when you say the phrase "sold out." Some may say this is a form of addiction or being obsessive.

What are you spending your time on? Because if it is with God, you are doing God's will. You cannot wait until Sunday comes to open your Bible. You cannot wait until Sunday comes to pray. You cannot wait until Sunday comes to say, "Thank You, Lord." What are you doing on Mondays, Tuesdays, Wednesdays, Thursdays, Fridays, and Saturdays? Time is what you need with Jesus. Time with Jesus is what you need to get your prayers answered. Time with Jesus will cause mountains to fall. "Sold out" is the type of relationship you need with God.

Can I share a little story with you? Many years ago, I met a woman who was once addicted to drugs. She was a mother of two beautiful daughters. She told me she had gotten involved with the wrong person, and her life went down the drain from that point. She told me she did things that no human being should never do, and she did it all for drugs. She lived under the bridge for two years, lost with no hope, but one day she had a moment of clarity, sitting on a bench at a bus stop. As she observed people getting on the bus and people getting off the bus, she remembered her mother waiting for her to get off the school bus in front of their house, and her mother would also greet her with a hug and a kiss. She sat on that bench until evening, thinking she needed her mother. She needed help, so she decided to go home to her mother. Despite her uncleanliness, her mother hugged her and kissed her and told her, "God heard my cry." Her mother told her she prayed every day, all day, fasting and reading God's words. She didn't care about time. She didn't care about staying up half of the night or all night, spending time with God and knowing God was the only way. This young lady is now living a normal life, free from drugs, and yes, her mother was "sold out" to Jesus.

So the praying doesn't cease. The praying increases, my people, because the devil is around somewhere, waiting to strike. I don't mean to sound nosy, but where are you on the sold-out scale, from one through ten? Where do you fit in, or do you fit on the scale at all? Matthew 6:24 says, "No one can serve two masters, for either he will hate the one and love the other, or he will be devoted to the one and despise the other." You cannot serve God and money. According to 1 John 2:15–17, "Do not love the world or the things in the world. If anyone loves the world, the love of the Father is not in him. For all that is in the world—the desire of the flesh and the desire of the eyes and pride in possession—is not from the Father but is from the world. And the world is passing away, along with its desires, but whoever does the will of God abides forever."

No one should wait until tomorrow to make a choice to follow Jesus. Your time is now. Please stop putting things off. Some of us live on procrastination. Stop! Look around. Tell me what you see.

Conclusion

Prayer Is Necessity

Our Father in heaven, hallowed be Your name. Your kingdom come, Your will be done on Earth as it is in heaven. Give us this day our daily bread and forgive us our debts as we forgive our debtors, and lead not into temptation but deliver us from evil, for thine is the kingdom and the power and the glory forever. Amen. (Matthew 6:9–13)

Every one of us has an obligation that must be fulfilled, and that is to pray, which is a vital part of God's purpose and God's will. Know that the will of God will flow from heaven to the earth only through God's prayer and of His people.

> But be ye doers of the word and not hearers only, deceiving your own selves. For if any be a hearer of the word and not a doer, he is like a man beholding his natural face in a glass. For he beholds himself and goes his way and straightaway forgets what manner of man he was. (James 1:22–24)

We must know that God wants us to approach Him as children. We are all God's children, and God must have a primary place in our lives because we were designed to find fulfillment and ultimate meaning in

God. Prayer builds intimacy with God. Prayer causes trust in His love. Prayer causes respect for God's integrity. Prayer is the key. Let me say this again. Prayer is the key. Without the key, the door won't ever open. We all have access to the key, but it is up to you to use the key. It is your choice. It is a decision you must make, but I truly hope it is God's way.

P.S. God is waiting for you, and His arms are open wide. "Come, my child."

About the Author

Alicia Jackson is first a mother of two beautiful children, Sandie and Devon, and second a grandmother of three lovable boys. She attended college and became a nurse and messenger of the Lord. She lived where everything is big—in the state of Texas, in a small town call Pflugerville, where her inspiration had first begun. She has just completed her second book, *Shacking with God*.

CPSIA information can be obtained
at www.ICGtesting.com
Printed in the USA
LVHW050226240720
661420LV00001B/171

9 781984 584465